MERE
HUMANITY

MERE HUMANITY

G. K. CHESTERTON, C. S. LEWIS, *and* J. R. R. TOLKIEN *on the* HUMAN CONDITION

DONALD T. WILLIAMS

BROADMAN
& HOLMAN
PUBLISHERS

NASHVILLE, TENNESSEE

Ten-Digit ISBN: 0-8054-4018-6
Thirteen-Digit ISBN: 978-0-8054-4018-8

Published by Broadman & Holman Publishers
Nashville, Tennessee

Dewey Decimal Classification: 233
Subject Heading: MAN (THEOLOGY) \ HUMANISM

1 2 3 4 5 6 7 8 9 10 11 12 13 14 15 15 14 13 12 11 10 09 08 07 06

*"Humanity practically was things that didn't have a position
in space and time;
such as imagination, pity, hope, history, and belief.
Take those away and all you had was an
ape that fell out of trees a lot."*
—Terry Pratchett, *Thief of Time*

*"Our primary business in life is not business,
or construction work, or sales, or teaching, or even motherhood,
but becoming a complete human being."*
—Peter Kreeft, *Back to Virtue*

*"What a piece of work is a man! How noble in reason!
How infinite in faculty!
In form and moving how express and admirable!
In action how like an angel!
In apprehension how like a god! The beauty of the world!
The paragon of animals! . . . We are arrant knaves all."*
—William Shakespeare, *Hamlet*

*"I will not call it my philosophy; for I did not make it.
God and humanity made it; and it made me."*
—G. K. Chesterton, *Orthodoxy*

CONTENTS

ACKNOWLEDGMENTS

Special thanks are due to Edie Dougherty and the Southern California C. S. Lewis Society, whose gracious invitation allowed the seed of what would become this book to germinate at their annual summer workshop at the Benedictine Abbey of Valyermo, California, some years ago. To the rich soil and gentle rain of their warm intellectual and spiritual companionship, the resulting plant owes much of whatever strength it may have.

A condensed version of the introduction and the first three chapters appeared as "'Is Man a Myth?': Mere Christian Perspectives on the Human," in *Mythlore*.[1] Part of chapter five appeared as "'Lions of Succession': Narnian Hierarchy and Human Relationships," in *Touchstone*.[2] A version of Appendix A appeared as "'A Larger World': C. S. Lewis on Christianity and Literature," in *Mythlore*.[3] A version of Appendix B appeared as "The Great Divide: The Church and the Post-Modernist Challenge," in *Christian Research Journal*.[4] I am grateful to all these publications for permission to reprint this material.

Friends and scholars such as Michael Bauman, Joe R. Christopher, Bruce L. Edwards, David Mills, Chris Mitchell, and Ted Sherman have read various parts of the manuscript and offered valuable suggestions. The errors which remain are manifestly my own.

THE BODY HUMAN

Intricate engine angels might admire,
   Material spirit, animated earth,
   Crafted casket for celestial fire,
   Doomed to die the day it has its birth.
Hands that open, befitting a gracious lord,
   Able to touch a cheek as soft as mist,
   To wield a pen, a brush, a harpsichord,
   But just as apt to freeze into a fist.
Godlike image, able to stand erect,
   Yet by what small and simple things laid low:
   A sneeze, a scratch, a germ, and all is wrecked;
   A few short years, the time has come to go.
Delicate instrument of love, or lust,
   Admirably compacted . . . out of dust.

—*D.T.W.*

Introduction

IS MAN A MYTH?

Mere Christian Perspectives on the Human

"What is this quintessence of dust?"

—HAMLET, IN SHAKESPEARE'S *HAMLET*

"IS MAN A MYTH?" asks the title of one of Mr. Tumnus's books. In his world of Narnia, it was apparently an open question until a certain daughter of Eve named Lucy showed up to have tea with him. The nature of the white witch's interest in the matter might have given him a clue to its answer, but still, until Lucy arrived, it was a debatable question. It may seem ironic, but the faun's question has become an open one again in the very world which Adam's and Eve's descendants are filling to the brim: not, that is, whether something called humanity exists but whether man, considered in the traditional way as something qualitatively different from the animals, uniquely created as God's child and steward of the planet and hence able to have definite and dependable ideas about his own identity and purpose, is not actually a mythical beast. In this book we will take this question seriously and attempt some steps toward an answer.

The Question

Its Nature and Difficulty

"What is man," the psalmist asked his God, "that you are mindful of him?" It was a good question and is a pressing one. Peter Kreeft lists it as one of the two most important questions we can ask: "What is man?" and "What is the purpose of his life on this earth?"[1] C. S. Lewis wisely observed that "the first qualification for judging any piece of workmanship from a corkscrew to a cathedral is to know what it is—what it was intended to do and how it is meant to be used."[2] In the case of mankind, this is especially true, for nothing else can be properly decided until we know the answer. *Metaphysics* (What is real?), *epistemology* (What can we know, and how do we know that we know it?), and *ethics* (What is the good?) are all affected, for it is we human beings who exist, who ask, and who choose. While other beings may also do these things, we have direct access to what they are like from the inside only as we do them ourselves. Hence, whatever concept of reality we have must be one that includes us. Any account of knowing that we accept must take into account the nature of the one attempting to know. And any definition of the good that guides us must be able to define what is good for precisely such beings as we discover ourselves to be, or it will be irrelevant to us.

The traffic between ourselves and these questions runs both ways. If we knew independently that only matter existed, for example, we would have to describe ourselves in purely materialistic terms. Everything we are, feel, know, and do would have to be completely describable in terms of atoms in motion. On the other hand, if we experience ourselves in ways that appear to transcend the purely physical, this would seem to tell us that some kind of metaphysical dualism must be true.[3]

So far, so good. But what if we seem to get one kind of answer when looking inward subjectively and another when trying to look outward with objectivity? In other words, what if we can't honestly reduce ourselves, as we know them from the inside, to nothing more than atoms in motion, but when we look out at the universe that is all we can objectively detect? It could be argued that this is precisely the position in which we find ourselves. As Marion Montgomery, summarizing Etienne Gilson, puts it, "We know, and know that we know, that life and *meaning* have real existence, though science cannot substantiate that reality because the reality at issue lies in a dimension of immateriality."[4]

No one feels his or her self to be nothing but atoms unless he or she has already been influenced by a dogmatic materialism.[5] Yet even materialists will try to convince you that materialism is *true,* which is inconsistent with their own position. For how can one arrangement of atoms ultimately produced by chance be more *true* than another such arrangement, equally produced by chance? In other words, how can the materialist's belief in materialism, described as the physical state of his brain (which, if he is right, is all that it is or can be) be more true than the dualist's opinion that there exists something else besides matter? Who stands outside both physical states to judge between them? For, in the materialist's view, that person's opinion is also a physical brain state ultimately produced, not by reason, but by the chance operations of the laws of physics. Giving chance the fancy, scientific-sounding title *evolution* really changes nothing. We must insist on asking the question of who is to judge between these beliefs? Or, more accurately, what is to judge? Another arrangement of atoms also inexorably produced by the impersonal workings-out of the laws of physics and chemistry? This leads us nowhere. Whatever the materialists say, they all *act* as if they thought they were more than chance collocations of atoms whenever (ironically) they make truth claims for materialism.[6]

This dilemma is an inescapable datum that I have tried to summarize thus:

THOUGHT

Villanelle no. 24

Whence comes a reason's power to convince,
  Illuminate the searching intellect
  With sudden serendipity of sense?
No change of chemicals or elements
  Could equal insight, letting us detect
  Whence comes a reason's power to convince.
Electrical impulses give no hints,
  Yield nothing that could cause us to expect
  A sudden serendipity of sense.
A chain of neurons firing boldly prints
  Its trace upon a screen which can't reflect
  Whence comes a reason's power to convince.
By faith we must accept this light that glints.
  The eye can't see itself, cannot inspect
  Its sudden serendipity of sense.
A mystery much like the sacraments
  Whose grace unseen we yet do not reject:
  Whence comes a reason's power to convince?
From sudden serendipity of sense.

—*D.T.W.*

Atoms in motion, in other words, simply cannot account for the fact that we know, perceive, and understand atoms in motion. They cannot even account for the fact that some of us think we *are* just atoms in motion, nor can they settle the disagreement between those who think so and the rest of us. They would have to be engaging in some rather peculiar motions were they to be able to do so. John Gardner defines consciousness as "the state in which not all atoms are equal. In corpses, entropy has won. The brain and the toenails have equal say."[7] If physics is the whole story about the universe, it is hard to see why they shouldn't always have equal say—or more accurately, why there should be any "say" to be had.

Yet it seems to be impossible directly to observe anything else except atoms in motion, whether because nothing else is there or because the seeing "eye can't see itself."[8] If spirit exists, we may think we experience it directly. But if we want that knowledge to become objective, then spirit apparently has to be inferred from its (material) effects.

Should we then privilege one of these visions over the other? Use one of them as the interpretive framework for explaining (or explaining away) the other? Which one? Why? You begin to see the difficulty of the question.

Its Importance

Nevertheless, as perplexing as the question is, we cannot not answer it; that is simply not an option that is open to us. In the first place, every person's life is lived in such a way as to imply an answer, whether it is consciously recognized and accepted as such or not. We cannot live a life that is not based on some answer, some concept of what humanity is and how it relates to the rest of reality; we can only live a life that does so in an examined or an unexamined way. And people who doubt the truth of Socrates's dictum that "the unexamined life is not worth living" only show that they have not really examined the issue.

Many other pressing questions also depend on the answer we give to this one. And the stakes are high.[9] How else could we know, to pick just one current and highly emotional issue: when and whether it is a good thing to terminate the uterine development of members of the human species whose conception has proved inconvenient. And how, if they are allowed to be born and to live, can we best educate them or govern them unless we know what kind of thing they are, what their nature is, what purposes (if any) they are meant to serve (by whom?), what they are for? Never have we known more about their physical makeup, their psychology, and their history; yet never have we been less confident about the answer all that information is meant to inform, which is certainly a precarious position for the race to find itself in. As Montaigne reminds us, "A man who has not directed his life as a whole toward a definite goal cannot possibly set his particular actions in order. A man who does not have a picture of the whole in his head cannot possibly arrange the pieces."[10]

So the question is obviously not an easy one, and it is as demanding as it is difficult. Whatever we may make of Pope's answer, he certainly recognized the complexity of the subject:

> *Placed on this isthmus of a middle state,*
> *A being darkly wise and rudely great:*
> *With too much knowledge for the Skeptic side,*
> *With too much weakness for the Stoic's pride,*
> *He hangs between; in doubt to act, or rest,*
> *In doubt to deem himself a God, or Beast;*
> *In doubt his Mind or Body to prefer,*
> *Born but to die, and reas'ning but to err;*
> *Alike in ignorance, his reason such,*
> *Whether he thinks too little or too much:*
> *Chaos of Thought and Passion all confused;*
> *Still by himself abused or disabused;*
> *Created half to rise and half to fall;*

Great lord of all things, yet a prey to all;
Sole judge of Truth, in endless Error hurled:
The glory, jest, and riddle of the world.
　　　　—*Alexander Pope,* An Essay on Man

Some Answers

Is man, as one venerable definition has it, a featherless biped? That answer, while certainly accurate, is surely inadequate. Is he a beast, a god, or a demon; or, with the advent of the couch potato, should we add vegetable to the list of options? Is he the most erected simian that climbed up out of the primordial ooze or the least erected spirit that fell from heaven? Is he a monkey with an opposable thumb or a marvel made in the image of God? According to the head agent in that intriguing movie *The Matrix,* it is wrong even to classify him as a mammal, for mammals find an equilibrium with their environment. But man multiplies heedlessly and uses up all the available resources, destroying the environment so that he has to expand to a new territory and repeat the process. Therefore, he should be classed with the only other species that lives in the same manner: the virus. Is man the measure of all things or just a measurement, a number, a statistic? Or is he, in the words of Sir Thomas Browne, "that great and true *amphibium,* whose nature is disposed to live, not only like other creatures in divers elements, but in divided and distinguished worlds?"[11] And how do we find out?

Two Paths

There have been two main approaches to trying to answer the question. Either may try to deal with both the inward and the outward visions described above, though they may end up evaluating them differently. Surely no answer that does not at least attempt to integrate both visions into one whole deserves consideration. (C. S. Lewis's essay "Meditation in a Toolshed" is an insightful discussion of this point.) The two approaches differ on the question of whether the inward and outward visions of humans *alone* are what must be considered; on whether, in other words, man is the only witness to his own nature that can be questioned. We might call them the secular and the religious ways.

The first is represented by Pope:

> *Know then thyself, presume not God to scan;*
> *The proper study of Mankind is Man.*

The second is that of Calvin: "Our wisdom, in so far as it ought to be deemed true and solid wisdom, consists almost entirely of two parts: the knowledge of God and of ourselves. But as these are connected together by many ties, it is not easy to determine which of the two precedes, and gives birth to the other."[12]

The first approach seems to manifest an admirable humility: Let's stay away from abstract and exalted theories and just deal with what we know, human experience. Just the facts, Ma'am. But what if God is one of the facts? Though this approach does not necessarily exclude God from existence, it does exclude him from relevance. And therefore, Pope's method actually arrogantly begs the question and commits us to a purely secular description of man "under the sun." Many views that go by religious names are essentially versions of this secular path, e.g., theological liberalism, as is shown when one of its fathers, Feuerbach, said that "theology is nothing else than anthropology—the knowledge of God nothing else than the knowledge of man."[13] We know the conclusion the author of Ecclesiastes reached when he tried the experiment of looking at us that way: "Vanity of vanities, saith the Preacher, vanity of vanities; all is vanity" (Eccles. 1:2 KJV).

The second approach seeks to understand man as related not just to the impersonal order of things but to Someone behind it. If we are indeed, as one major tradition insists, created in the image of God, then we cannot be understood at all except in that context. This method would carry its own kind of arrogance if indeed we thought we could presume to "scan" the infinite—unless, that is, the divine had taken the initiative and revealed himself to us, which is precisely what Christians claim has happened in Christ, the place where Calvin's quests for knowledge of God and of man come together.

How then ought we to proceed, since each path of inquiry seems already at the outset committed to a certain kind of answer? Perhaps the best procedure is to explore them both together and then ask which one leads us to the place where we actually find ourselves. Because man is the only object of study that we know from the inside as well as the outside, that is a question we just might be able to answer.

We are surrounded by profoundly trivial examples of what lies at the end of Pope's path. If there is one God, matter, and science is its prophet, then we should expect to be completely satisfied by "material girls" who want to "just get physical," by soulless yuppies who actually seem to believe that he who dies with the most toys wins. If people find such an approach to life deeply fulfilling, if when lying awake alone in bed at night they feel not the slightest urge to ask, "Is that all there is?" then they have their answer, and I need trouble them no further. But if, though they hardly ever dare be vulnerable enough to admit it, there is something deep within that remains empty for all that matter can do; if, when they do look at humanity long and hard and honestly from the inside, they are forced to admit that the material and temporal can titillate and entertain, can distract life from pain for awhile but cannot justify its existence, then I would beg leave to suggest an alternative.

Mere Christian Pilgrims

Three thinkers with strangely kindred and interconnected minds (two were friends, both influenced by the first) make the best guides we could ask for in such a journey. One of the most fertile minds of the early twentieth century tried the experiment of looking at man as an animal and discovered that there was no more fearful wildfowl than your human living, that to make this attempt proves that we are spirits of a different sort. Two of the most fertile minds of the middle of the century built on that work in rich and incisive ways. The three were G. K. Chesterton, C. S. Lewis, and J. R. R. Tolkien.

Chesterton laid the foundations of this Christian anthropology in what many consider his greatest work, *The Everlasting Man*. Lewis developed it in the light of midcentury secularist attacks in *The Abolition of Man,* and then incarnated it in a series of fictional works set in other worlds. By contrasting human beings with other *hnau*—rational/spiritual animals—and with *eldila*—spiritual beings—in the Space Trilogy, he brings into focus the essential quiddity of humanity that he and Chesterton had expounded. The relations between human beings, sons of Adam and daughters of Eve, and the talking beasts of The Chronicles of Narnia have the same effect. Elves, dwarves, orcs, and hobbits are the foils which allowed Tolkien to achieve a similar setting off of human characteristics in *The Hobbit* and The Lord of the Rings trilogy. And we will discover that, while each of these writers had his own emphases, it is a common and unified vision of humanity that they ultimately offer us.

So now we may clamber onto the shoulders of those giants as we attempt to peer into the new millennium. Marion Montgomery has said that "literature provides texts to which theology applies philosophy."[14] His critical epigram defines with admirable precision the kind of peering we will be trying to do. We will make no attempt to produce a systematic anthropology (like Wheeler Robinson's, for example). We will still not know when we are through whether dichotomy or trichotomy is the correct view of the interrelationships of body, soul, and spirit. Our concern is not with such technicalities but rather with the larger view of man's nature and purpose and with the human condition as it is portrayed in a series of insightful literary texts that fruitfully embody an old and wise philosophy. "Is man a myth?" we will ask. Perhaps not, we will discover; but there was a time when a myth became a man.

Interlude

APOLOGIA

Structured steps within the dance,
Things which could not be by chance;
Architecture of belief?
Arch of bole and vein of leaf.
Crystal's angles; raindrop's curves;
Bone and sinew knit with nerves.
Flick of wrist, fly-toss, and then
Break of bubble, flash of fin.
Beyond these sure and certain hints,
A clearer class of evidence:
Broken fever, opened eyes,
Dove descending from the skies.
Footstep firm on slope of wave;
Stone rolled back from Jesus' grave.
Glory growing out of grief?
Architecture of belief;
Things that could not be by chance:
Structured steps within the dance.

—*D.T.W.*

Chapter One

CHESTERTON AND THE EVERLASTING MAN

*"There are more things in heaven and
earth, Horatio, than are dreamt of in your
philosophy."*

—HAMLET, IN SHAKESPEARE'S *HAMLET*

IF WE TAKE POPE'S secular path to understanding man, we will
of necessity view him as an animal: a chimpanzee with less hair, an
opposable thumb, and a more flexible jaw, as it were. For the only
viable destination which lies down Pope's path for modern people
is an evolutionary model. Man would be a simple extension of what
is seen in the animal kingdom, produced by the same (ultimately
irrational) processes and adapted to the same (ultimately impersonal)
ends. He would necessarily therefore differ from what we observe in
the other animals only in degree, not in kind.[1] Whether we found it
so could possibly give us an external and objective way of confirming
our inward and subjective intuition that we must be more than just
atoms in motion. As John Gardner's Grendel observes, animals "see
all life without observing it. They are buried in it like crabs in mud.

Except men, of course."[2] The mere fact that human beings are the
ones asking the question implies which way the answer should go.

It should be noted, by the way, that I am taking no position
about how far the theory of evolution can go toward explaining
human origins, other than to insist that it cannot be the whole story.[3]
The theory of natural selection undoubtedly works on a small scale
(what is sometimes called "micro-evolution"), explaining variations
within a species. Whether this process can actually transmute one
species into another is more doubtful. The cynical dragon in John
Gardner's *Grendel* pictures the universe, like many secularists, as
"a swirl in the stream of time. A temporary gathering of bits, a few
random dust specks," which by pure accident pick up "refinements:
sensitive dust, copulating dust, *worshipful dust!*"[4] Is this view even
plausible outside a prior commitment to naturalism? I have my opin-
ions on questions such as young-Earth versus old-Earth creationism,
but this is not the place to rehearse them. My only business here is to
question whether naturalistic evolution can succeed as an adequate
explanation of the uniqueness of man, for that is a question that
Chesterton raises rather insistently.

One of the curious facts about naturalistic evolutionary theory is
that, while evolutionists seem committed to it and will defend it to the
death against creationists, they do not really seem to take it all that seriously. They will claim that we are only another animal and then tell us it
is unethical for us to be a predatory species. They will tell us that evolution (which somehow acquires a capital letter in tone if not in actuality)
works by the survival of the fittest, and then they demand scrupulous
honesty from other researchers and are horrified by the predations of
robber-baron capitalists. They seem curiously loath to pursue their own
premises to their logical conclusions. It was Chesterton's contribution in
his apologetic masterpiece *The Everlasting Man* to take this evolutionary
idea more seriously than its own proponents did in order to see if it could
really be made to work.

What Chesterton discovered in this experiment was that "it is exactly when we do regard man as an animal that we know he is not an animal."[5] His evidence for this conclusion is given in a series of impressionistic brushstrokes that add up to a compelling portrait behind which is hidden a linear argument known as the *reductio ad absurdum* ("reduction to absurdity": one accepts one's opponent's premises for the sake of argument and pushes them to their logical conclusions to show that they are contradictory). His brilliant mind darts about the intellectual landscape like a hummingbird.[6] The flight may at times seem erratic, but he never forgets either what nectar he is seeking or where his nest is.

"George Wyndham once told me," he notes, "that he had seen one of the first aeroplanes rise for the first time and it was very wonderful; but not so wonderful as a horse allowing a man to ride on him."[7] What is so wonderful about this? Rhinoceri allow tickbirds, sharks remora to ride on them, but the very analogies self-destruct as defenses of the evolutionary approach. These other symbiotic relationships are instinctual, and the relationship between man and horse anything but. Rhinoceri are not directed by tickbirds whither they shall go by bit and bridle and the pressure of knees. Wherever the two species are found, moreover, the birds are found upon the backs. But it did not occur to all men at all times that horses could be persuaded to bear them, nor have all horses at all times been so persuaded. And while the word *persuaded* is no doubt a metaphor, it is a singularly apt metaphor. Even where men and horses have been performing this exotic behavior together for centuries, it does not come naturally to either species but has to be learned by both. When the first man thought of the idea, it was not a linear evolutionary projection from anything nature had done before but an outlandish notion that was probably laughed to scorn until he actually pulled it off. And while our species has a long history of coming up with such outlandish notions that for good or evil veer straight off into space from anything that evolution could project, nobody will seriously argue that the horse was the one first to propose riding in exchange for warm stalls, currycombs, and oats. Why not?

The Signature of Man

Chesterton does not stop to elucidate his observation as I have done; he is off to look at another flower. But there is one kind of blossom he keeps circling back to: "It is the simple truth that man does differ from the brutes in kind and not in degree; and the proof of it is here; that it sounds like a truism to say that the most primitive man drew a picture of a monkey and that it sounds like a joke to say that the most intelligent monkey drew a picture of a man. Something of division and disproportion has appeared; and it is unique. Art is the signature of man."[8]

The most primitive forms of humanity that we have uncovered manifest this amazing trait, and the most advanced forms of the other species do not. "After all, it would come back to this; that he had dug very deep and found the place where a man had drawn the picture of a reindeer. But he would dig a good deal deeper before he found a place where a reindeer had drawn a picture of a man."[9]

Art is the signature of man. Or, as Kilby nicely puts it, it is his "lengthened shadow."[10] Once again, analysis only deepens and widens this chasm between us and the other species. Monkeys may sharpen sticks to make primitive tools for digging termites out of the ground; they may arrange boxes into a pile they can climb to retrieve a banana hung from the ceiling. They do not arrange the sticks or the boxes into intricate patterns simply so they can sit back and lose themselves in the contemplation of their symmetry. Other species, in other words, pursue the practical arts on a rudimentary level but know nothing of what we call the fine arts. And this impulse to "fine" (or what we might better call "unnecessary") art in the human species extends itself to touch all the practical arts as well; in fact, it may be most impressive there:

> The very fact that a bird can get as far as building a nest, and cannot get any farther, proves that he has not a mind as man has a mind; it proves it more completely than if he built nothing at all. If he built nothing at all, he might possibly be a philosopher of the Quietist or Buddhistic school, indifferent to all but the mind within. But when he builds as he does build and is satisfied and sings aloud with satisfaction, then we know there is really an invisible veil like a pane of glass between him and us, like the window on which a bird will beat in vain. But suppose our abstract onlooker saw one of the birds begin to build as men build. Suppose in an incredibly short space of time there were seven styles of architecture for one style of nest. Suppose the bird carefully selected forked twigs and pointed leaves to express the piercing piety of Gothic, but turned to broad foliage and black mud when he sought in a darker mood to call up the heavy columns of Bel and Ashtaroth; making his nest indeed one of the hanging gardens of Babylon. Suppose the bird made little clay statues of birds celebrated in letters or politics and stuck them up in front of the nest. Suppose that one bird out of a thousand birds began to do one of the thousand things that man had already done even in the morning of the world; and we can be quite certain that the onlooker would not regard such a bird as a mere evolutionary variety of the other birds; he would regard it as a very fearful wild-fowl indeed.[11]

Reductionisms

Once we give up the idea that humanity was uniquely created in the image of God, it is hard to find a rationale for this difference, and the temptation arises to try to explain it away so that our naturalistic philosophies are not threatened by it. One strategy for this explaining away is *reductionism*: every part of reality is reduced to—that is, must be explained in terms of—one arbitrarily privileged other part. Because this strategy unifies a great many of the views we will be examining in this study and thus constitutes one of the more important concepts we will be using, we need to make sure we understand it. While there are many forms of reductionism, they are all ultimately related, as Newman explains:

> This view has been given various names, depending on the nuance in mind. As an absolutizing of science to be the only means to true knowledge, it is called "scientism" [see Aeschliman for a fine treatment of this issue]. As the claim that matter/energy is the ultimate reality, it is called "materialism." As the belief that everything can be explained by the operation of purely natural forces without miracles at all, it is called "naturalism." As the view that all the complex organization in our universe has developed by unguided processes working within natural laws, it is called "evolutionism."[12]

We might add that as the view that only time, as opposed to eternity, exists and is relevant to human affairs, it is called "secularism," from the Latin *saeculum*, "time" or "age."[13] That is why Richard Weaver says that "modernism is in essence a provincialism, since it declines to look beyond the horizon of the moment, just as the countryman may view with suspicion whatever lies beyond his country."[14]

A person who accepts any one of these forms will logically tend to be, and usually will be, a proponent also of the others[15] and also of subjectivism.[16] They all are unified in essentially reducing everything in the universe to atoms in motion.[17] Once you have done that on the cosmic level, your mind will naturally gravitate to reductionist explanations of more limited topics, i.e., reducing all human motivation and behavior to sex (Freudianism), economics (Marxism), conditioning (Behaviorism), or power (Nietzsche).

The many different ways in which people try to reduce the vast complexity of life to one thing should make us suspicious of the whole process. But it is not just counterintuitive; Polanyi has shown that reductionism is invalid on a theoretical level. As we move from physics to mechanics to biology to personality, each level is inherently "unspecifiable in terms of the lower."[18] A person who knew the disposition, direction, and speed of every atomic particle in the universe could not on this basis explain a simple machine, for machines include a factor that does not exist in the Laplacean analysis: they were designed for a purpose. As a mechanism is more than the sum of its atoms, so a living creature is more than the sum of its mechanisms and a person more than the sum of its organic processes. Polanyi would seem to have shown that this refutation of reductionism is inescapable. The failure to realize this foundational truth gives a family resemblance to all reductionistic explanations. Therefore, when we have occasion to refer to any of these manifestations it should be seen as related to the whole complex, for they do form a naturally unified way of looking at the world.

When Chesterton questions the ability of evolution to explain the phenomenon of man, then, he is seeing it, even if he does not use that term, not simply as a scientific theory which may explain some things about natural processes but as a form of reductionism and one that logically flows from the loss of the Christian worldview.[19] Christian faith and reductionism are in this sense mutually exclusive alternatives; reductionistic explanations of human nature rise as a robust understanding and acceptance of Christian belief falls. As early as the end of the Renaissance, Montaigne was wondering whether any valid distinction could be made between himself and his cat, who quite possibly regarded him as just as much a plaything as he did her.[20] Knowing cats, we can say that she probably did, but what does that prove? Montaigne doubted the radical distinction between man and cat because there were so many human behaviors that had analogies in the beasts: building, hunting, caring for young, etc. Which of our arts, he asked, do we not find there?[21]

Today we even wonder the same thing about machines[22] fascinated with the possibilities of artificial intelligence (AI). From C3PO and R2D2 to Commander Data, robots and androids are among our favorite science fiction characters, and a new attitude toward them is emerging. In *Star Trek*'s first generation, Mr. Spock as the voice of reason objected to the M-5 Unit's taking over the *Enterprise*, arguing that "computers make excellent servants, but I have no wish to serve under them." By the next generation, Commander Data—confessedly a machine whose "positronic brain" is simply a complex computer—holds a commission in Starfleet, and human beings routinely serve under him. Captain Picard defends him in a hearing at which it is determined that there is no reason not to grant him full human rights.

What machines that we have created in our own image will be capable of in the future remains to be seen, though Roger Penrose has argued persuasively that real personality in them is not mathematically possible. But the distinction between man and animal can be lost only if we limit ourselves to observing and cataloging the practical arts. "What is a man," Hamlet perceptively asks, "if his chief good and market of his time / be but to sleep and feed? A beast, no more." Watching monkeys sharpen their sticks as primitive toolmakers can blind us to the fact that monkeys who started arranging their sticks into symmetrical patterns for no pragmatic purpose would be strange monkeys indeed. Analogies to human arts in the animal kingdom, in other words, serve only to reinforce Chesterton's conclusion that we are looking across a vast chasm which evolution alone could not bridge and, in fact, has not bridged. Birds do not gather to listen to the songs of other birds for pleasure or fulfillment, nor do they sing to express sorrow or joy but rather to tell the other birds to stay the heck out of their territory. What we call birdsong is "song" only after it has been filtered through a human mind. Art is the signature of man because it constitutes a radical break with animal behavior, not a development from it: "There is in fact not a trace of any such development or degree. Monkeys did not begin pictures and men finish them; Pithecanthropus did not draw a reindeer badly and Homo Sapiens draw it well. The higher animals did not draw better and better portraits; the dog did not paint better in his best period than in his early bad manner as a jackal; the wild horse was not an Impressionist and the race-horse a Post-Impressionist."[23]

The Irreducible Mind

The arts, in other words, show that man is not merely adaptive, like the animals, but more than that: he is creative. "This creature was truly different from all other creatures; because he was a creator as well as a creature."[24] He is not merely responsive to his environment; he initiates new things not dreamt of in nature's philosophy. He is able to do this because he acts not from instinct but from understanding; he has an irresistible urge to try to see things in terms of principles. He has, therefore, in a sense not shared by the other animals, a mind. He is that creature who is therefore uniquely accountable to the Mind which gave him that mind for what Marion Montgomery calls "a deportment of intellect governed by a continuing concern for the truth of things."[25] Ironically, science itself can only be a valid path to truth, that is, be a part of that required deportment of the intellect, if it does not try to be the *only* valid path, if, in other words, it depends on something it cannot

image of God?

itself dissect. Moreland explains, "Many of the presuppositions of science (e.g. the existence of truth, the rationality and orderly nature of reality, the adequacy of our sensory and cognitive faculties as tools suited for knowing the external world) make sense and are easy to justify given Christian theism, but are odd and without justification in a naturalistic worldview."[26]

And there is something in these facts that is more than natural, if philosophy could find it out. For on naturalistic principles, it is a thing that ought not to be. So Chesterton says, "No philosopher denies that a mystery still attaches to the two great transitions: the origin of the universe itself and the origin of the principle of life itself. Most philosophers have the enlightenment to add that a third mystery attaches to the origin of man himself. In other words, a third bridge was built across a third abyss of the unthinkable when there came into the world what we call reason and what we call will. Man is not merely an evolution but rather a revolution."[27]

We know that evolution is, at most, less than the whole truth about us because the mind of man, as Chesterton has observed it, is something it could not have produced. The assumption that it could result from mere inattention to the reality of who we are as developed above, driven perhaps by reductionist philosophies that focus only on the physical. "There may be a broken trail of stones and bones faintly suggesting the development of the human body. There is nothing even faintly suggesting such a development of this human mind. It was not and it was; we know not in what instant or in what infinity of years. Something happened; and it has all the appearance of a transaction outside time."[28]

The Philosophy of Stories

One either allows for a transaction from outside of time, or one is left with a secularist reductionism. Various forms of such reductionism—

economic, psychological, sexual—have naturally been the dominant paradigms for processing human experience in our secular age, as Marxism, Freudianism, and later postmodern forms of race/class/ gender-based literary criticism attest.[29] And they are all ultimately dehumanizing, leaving out of the story much of what makes it worth telling. "Cows," Chesterton continues, "may be purely economic, in the sense that we cannot see that they do much beyond grazing and seeking better grazing grounds; and that is why a history of cows in twelve volumes would not be very lively reading."[30] Why is the story of humanity, appalling though it often is, very lively reading indeed? Because secularism *is* reductionism, and man, even secular man, will not be so reduced: "The story only begins where the motive of the cows and sheep leaves off. It will be hard to maintain that the Crusaders went from their homes into a howling wilderness because cows go from a wilderness to a more comfortable grazing-ground. It will be hard to maintain that the Arctic explorers went north with the same material motive that made the swallows go south. And if you leave things like all the religious wars and all the merely adventurous explorations out of the human story, it will not only cease to be human at all but cease to be a story at all."[31]

The human story nevertheless stays a *story* for all that reductionist philosophy and criticism can do and thereby hangs a tale, one that, Chesterton suggests, ought to tell us something. The fact that we tell stories is significant because it flows from the fact that we *are* a story. We might call this the Narrative Argument for Theism: as a contingent universe needs a Creator, a dynamic universe needs an unmoved Mover, an intelligent and orderly universe needs a Designer, and a moral universe needs a Lawgiver, so a universe containing a creature whose life is utterly inexplicable except as a story demands a Storyteller. Without reference to him, there is no explanation for this creature except reductionisms of whatever sort.

We know therefore where Chesterton is going: the only explanation of humanity that actually explains it is the one that says we are
adventurous because we are a venture, that we are creative and mindful because we were created in the image of the Creator who is still, as
the psalmist marvels, mindful of us. Ultimately nothing less than full
Christian orthodoxy allows man to be fully human. Western secular
philosophies reduce him to an animal or a machine, and Eastern religious ones to nothingness. "I maintain that when brought out into
the daylight these two things look altogether strange and unique. . . .
The first of these is the creature called man, and the second is the
man called Christ."[32] They look strange, that is, when we come to
them with either secular or pantheistic presuppositions yet without
letting those assumptions blind us to the full reality of what they are.
This, of course, is difficult to do while we are still in the grip of those
stifling ideologies. It needs a thinker who has already outgrown them
to show us the way. It is Chesterton's ability to do just that which
makes him so valuable.

We need not follow here all the details of how our darting
hummingbird zeroes in on Bible and creed as the foundations of
anthropology. It has much to do with the plentiful lack of plot in
the history of cows in twelve volumes, together with the fact that
the Bible gives us the plot that makes sense of us, hence providing
a foundation for what Chesterton calls "the philosophy of stories."[33]
Once the plausibility of naturalism has been exploded, the rest of the
path is fairly plain. And once Chesterton has opened our eyes to it, his
conclusion strikes with inevitable force: "It is not natural to see man
as a natural product."[34] Man is the only one of the physical creatures
with enough of a self to want to sign his name; art is his signature,
and he gets both from the greatest Artist of all.

Interlude

HERE'S THE MARVEL

Here's the marvel: that the self-contained
  And all-sufficient triple Unity
  Which for untold eternities had reigned
  Complete in its own pure simplicity
Should will unnecessary worlds to be.
  And yet his mind was steel, his purpose flint:
  He struck off sparks of flaming ecstasy
  And called the stars by name. The thing he meant?
To make his glory visible. He sent
  Forth pulsing space-time-matter-energy
  Which danced in pirouettes as on it went.
  Just one thing more was needed: eyes to see
And skin to feel, and mind to comprehend.
  He called it Adam, and there made an end.
                    —D.T.W.

Chapter Two

C. S. LEWIS AND THE ABOLITION OF MAN

"Oh, brave new world that has such people in it!"

—MIRANDA, IN SHAKESPEARE'S *THE TEMPEST*

CHESTERTON, BY TAKING THE secular approach more seriously than the secularists, made it collapse into absurdity. But not everyone was serious enough to laugh with him. Another generation passed, the effects of reductionism proceeded apace, and by midcentury the farsighted had begun to wonder whether our insistence on seeing man as merely an animal might become so addictive that we would lose the ability to function as more. If the human *differentia* came, as Chesterton argued, from God, they could hardly be abolished.[1] But still we could try and in trying do a great deal of damage. So we move, in an ironic procession of titles, from Chesterton's *The Everlasting Man* to C. S. Lewis's *The Abolition of Man,* a book in which he charts the form those reductionistic efforts were taking by midcentury and responds to them so forcefully that he is singled out by B. F. Skinner in his reductionist manifesto as one of the champions of the "literatures of freedom and dignity."[2] This characterization, intended by Skinner as dismissive, is to those who do not share his reductionist presuppositions both an accurate description and a high accolade indeed.

The Abolition of Education

Changes in our view of human nature inevitably show up in educational theory and practice, even if they are not articulated there as such. So Lewis begins by being concerned about language he finds in a book for teaching English to schoolchildren. It was *The Control of Language,* by Alec King and Martin Ketley,[3] but Lewis charitably disguises the authors as Gaius and Titius and refers to their volume as *The Green Book.* "Gaius and Titius comment as follows: 'When that man said *That is sublime,* he appeared to be making the remark about the waterfall. . . . Actually . . . he was not making a remark about the waterfall, but a remark about his own feelings.'"[4] In this seemingly innocent observation, Lewis smells nothing less than the Giant Rat of Sumatra. "The schoolboy who reads this passage in *The Green Book* will believe two propositions: firstly, that all sentences containing a predicate of value are statements about the emotional state of the speakers, and, secondly, that all such statements are unimportant."[5]

What happens when we switch from statements about the aesthetic beauty of waterfalls to statements about moral values or about the value of human life? If naturalism is true, then only the physically quantifiable is real. So if we are taught to treat only the physically quantifiable as real, then we have created a presumption that naturalism is true. And that presumption digs an unbridgeable chasm between us and the whole history of human experience and understanding. "Good and ill have not changed since yesteryear; nor are they one thing among Elves and Dwarves and another among Men," said Aragorn,[6] speaking with the united voice of the race before the advent of late modernism.

The *Tao*

Lewis explains the meaning and implications of Aragorn's view: "Until quite modern times all teachers and even all men believed the universe to be such that certain emotional reactions on our part could be either congruous or incongruous to it—believed, in fact, that objects did not merely receive, but could *merit,* our approval or disapproval, our reverence, or our contempt."[7] They felt that way because, having not yet accepted the premise that only the physically quantifiable is real, they were free to believe in the reality of other than numerical values. Lewis calls this traditional approach to life "the doctrine of objective value," and the hierarchy of values perceived in the universe in the light of it the *Tao.* "It is the doctrine of objective value, the belief that certain attitudes are really true, and others really false, to the kind of thing the universe is and the kind of things we are. Those who know the *Tao* can hold that to call children delightful or old men venerable is not simply to record a psychological fact about our own parental or filial emotions at the moment, but to recognize a quality which *demands* a certain response from us whether we make it or not."[8]

He gives a similar analysis in *The Four Loves,* noticing that "when Need-Pleasures are in question we tend to make statements about ourselves in the past tense; when Appreciative Pleasures are in question we tend to make statements about the object in the present tense."[9] There are certain pleasures, in other words, that are dependent on our subjective condition: nobody really enjoys a glass of water unless he is thirsty, after which he may exclaim, "I needed that!" But there are others which are not so dependent in quite the same way, beauties in nature, for example, which we were not consciously looking for but which hit us out of the blue as something that "has not merely gratified our senses in fact but claimed our appreciation by right."[10] The person passing by a row of sweet peas "does not simply enjoy, he feels that this fragrance somehow deserves to be enjoyed. He would blame himself if he went past inattentive and undelighted. It would be blockish, insensitive."[11]

The only alternative to accepting the *Tao* is some form of subjectivism, an approach that is increasingly attractive to our contemporaries. As Packer explains: "Subjectivism appears as a call to cast off the shackles of the past by relativizing yesterday's absolutes, which sounds like a siren song inviting us to freedom; but the effect is to turn each individual into a cultural castaway, rootless and directionless, a voyager lost in the cosmos. By undermining the moral authority of our communal heritage and telling us that, whatever we do, we must not be bound by it, subjectivism impoverishes us most grievously."[12] That is why, as with the sublimity of the waterfall, Lewis is not willing to have any of these reactions, even the purely aesthetic ones, reduced to mere subjective responses. "You can 'kill' the finest mountain prospect by locating it all in your own retina and optic nerves."[13] To him they are rather keys to something true about the universe. And why shouldn't they be? For they are consistent with what he discovered through his use of the Moral Argument for Theism in *Mere Christianity*: values of any kind are not as reducible to mathematics, biology, or culture as modern (or postmodern)[14] secular thought would have us believe.[15] The *Tao* is inescapable in morals *or* aesthetics.

Humanity and the *Tao*

The humanity of the human species, those qualities that according to Chesterton separate us from the merely animal, depends on the existence of this objective but not physical *Tao* and our ability to perceive it. If only the physically quantifiable is real, then the evolutionary model is an adequate description of us, and man's uniqueness is an illusion. But if naturalism is false, if we are creative minds because we were created by the ultimate Mind, then values are not merely subjective. The valuations made by the Creator himself have the same reality as the physical objects he made and which he values, and discovering those values is the path to fulfillment for humans who want their lives to have value as well. As Augustine put it: "Everything God created is good. The rational soul performs good action when it observes the order of creation, when it chooses the greater over the lesser, the higher over the lower, spiritual values over material goods, eternal realities over those that only last in time."[16]

If this is true, then Milton's Satan—and the hordes of modern and postmodern thinkers who follow him—are wrong when they claim that "the mind is its own place, and in itself / can make a heaven of hell, a hell of heaven."[17] No. The mind, like every other place, is God's place, and will function fruitfully only when it bows to the reality that God has made. Heaven is not hell, nor hell heaven, just because the mind says it is. In other words, the existence of this *Tao* over and above the mind means that there is the potential for a rational, not merely an instinctual, grounding for what humans value and how they feel about it: "Because our approvals and disapprovals are thus recognitions of objective value or responses to an objective order, therefore emotional states can be in harmony with reason (when we feel liking for what ought to be approved) or out of harmony with reason (when we perceive that liking is due but cannot feel it)."[18]

Lewis does not at this point specify the Christian theistic grounding of the *Tao*; he saves that task, in effect, for *Mere Christianity* and *Miracles*, being here content to appeal to the universal perception of the *Tao* in premodern times that he documents in the appendix.[19] What he zeroes in on is the fact that modern secularist reductionism, by defining the *Tao* out of existence and insisting that nothing but the physically quantifiable can be real or objective, also rules out of court precisely the central essence of human nature.

The peculiarity of that nature is that humanity is indeed located squarely on Pope's "isthmus of a middle state." This much Pope had retained of the tradition. We are that being that, like the animals, has a physical body influenced by instinct but, like the angels, has a spiritual nature capable of perceiving the *Tao*. The reality of our animal nature provides plenty of evidence for those who would reduce us to that nature alone (as we saw with Montaigne in the chapter on Chesterton), but the uniqueness of our position in creation is that, as far as we know, we are the only creature that has to deal with the sometimes difficult integration of that animal nature with the spiritual. "We are composite creatures, rational animals, akin on one side to the angels, on the other to tom-cats";[20] we are "that great and true *amphibium,* whose nature is disposed to live not only like other creatures in divers elements but in divided and distinguished worlds."[21] Lewis recognized this aspect of our situation and stressed its importance for how we conceive the process of education, specifically the danger of ignoring it:

> We were told it all long ago by Plato. As the king governs
> by his executive, so Reason in man must rule the mere
> appetites by means of the "spirited element." The head
> rules the belly through the chest—the seat, as Alanus tells
> us, of Magnanimity, of emotions organized by trained
> habit into stable sentiments. The Chest—Magnanimity—
> Sentiment—these are the indispensable liaison officers
> between cerebral man and visceral man. It may even be
> said that it is by this middle element that man is man: for
> by his intellect he is mere spirit and by his appetite mere
> animal. The operation of *The Green Book* and its kind is to
> produce what may be called Men without Chests.[22]

The *Tao* perceived by the mind, in other words, is not automatically followed by the body. That is what it means to have a mind rather than operating by mere instinct. So part of the role of education is to foster well-ordered emotions, sentiments that aid the mind in governing the body according to the *Tao*. It is, in other words, to transmit to the next generation the developed ways of feeling about things that have been discovered by the sometimes bitter experience of many previous generations to be in accordance with reason and the *Tao*—to transmit civilization. If we insist that thoughts about values are really only feelings, and then debunk feelings about values as baseless because the values cannot be stuck into either a test tube or a calculator, we foster barbarism instead. And as human beings, neither animal nor angel, we need both the thoughts and the feelings. "Without the aid of trained emotions the intellect is powerless against the animal organism. I had sooner play cards against a man who was quite skeptical about ethics, but bred to believe that 'a gentleman does not cheat,' than against an irreproachable moral philosopher who had been brought up among sharpers."[23]

Education in the spirit of *The Green Book*, in the spirit of reductionist materialism, trains something that is less than human. Because of the way it denies or devalues the mind (reducing it to the brain), it leaves out entirely the middle element, seeing no necessity to integrate something that transcends the physical with a physical nature conceived as the whole person. (Attempts to deal with teen-age pregnancy through that oxymoronic method of "values-free" sex education come to mind.) As Lewis describes it, "In a sort of ghastly simplicity we remove the organ and demand the function. We make men without chests and expect of them virtue and enterprise. We laugh at honour and are shocked to find traitors in our midst. We castrate and bid the geldings be fruitful."[24] It is then impossible to overestimate what is at stake in these rival conceptions of human nature. "The practical result of education in the spirit of *The Green Book* must be the destruction of the society which accepts it."[25]

The Abolition of Man

We cannot make human beings less than human; but by training them to think of themselves as less than human, we can get them to act as less, with disastrous consequences. In other words, we may not be able to make them unhuman, but we can make them inhuman.[26] Therefore, Lewis speaks with hyperbole perhaps but nevertheless makes a valid point when he says of those who operate on the basis of materialist reductionism that "it is not that they are bad men. They are not men at all. Stepping outside the *Tao*, they have stepped into the void."[27] They have tried with mixed success to give up something that is essential to full humanity, at least. The two rival conceptions of humanity stare at each other across a great chasm, and what is at stake is the possibility of a civilization in which man can be whole, develop to his full potential: "Either we are rational spirit obliged for ever to obey the absolute values of the *Tao*, or else we are mere nature to be kneaded and cut into new shapes for the pleasures of masters who must, by hypothesis, have no motive but their own 'natural' impulses. Only the *Tao* provides a common human law of action which can overarch rulers and ruled alike. A dogmatic belief in objective value is necessary to the very idea of a rule which is not tyranny or an obedience which is not slavery."[28]

Its Ultimate Impossibility

In summary, to be human is to be an animal who is more, who has also a spiritual nature and is therefore aware of and accountable to follow spiritual values. Though reductionists deny the existence of such creatures, implying that man in that sense is in fact a myth, they themselves cannot escape the *Tao*. For they think that we *ought* to reject traditional values as an impediment to human progress; but if they are right, the word *ought* is meaningless. In a materialist world no manipulation of any of the ciphers properly admitted to that world could ever possibly produce such a concept. "If he had really started from scratch, from right outside the human tradition of value, no jugglery could have advanced him an inch towards the conception that a man should die for the community or work for posterity. If the *Tao* falls, all his own conceptions of value fall with it. Not one of them can claim any authority other than that of the *Tao*. Only by such shreds of the *Tao* as he has inherited is he enabled even to attack it."[29]

Or, in other words:

[The *Tao*] is not one among a series of possible systems of value. It is the sole source of all value judgements. If it is rejected, all value is rejected. If any value is retained, it is retained. The effort to refute it and raise a new system of value in its place is self-contradictory. There never has been, and never will be, a radically new judgement of value in the history of the world. What purport to be new systems or (as they now call them) "ideologies," all consist of fragments from the *Tao* itself, arbitrarily wrenched from their context in the whole and then swollen to madness in their isolation, yet still owing to the *Tao* and to it alone such validity as they possess.[30]

Lewis illustrates this point in *Out of the Silent Planet,* when Oyarsa, the governing spirit of Malacandra, diagnoses Weston's "bentness" as proceeding from the fact that there are laws known to all *hnau* (the Old Solar word for "sentient animal"), including pity, straight dealing, and love of kindred. But Weston has taken the love of kindred, a true law in itself, out of its context in the *Tao* and made it into "a little, blind Oyarsa in your brain."[31] As a result, he breaks all the other laws and does not even truly keep that one, for he is willing to sacrifice any individual human being for what he considers the abstract good of the race. Even Weston can be evil, not by creating new values apart from the *Tao* but only by truncating and twisting the ones it gives us. Because the hierarchy of value God has placed in the world is an objective reality, "The human mind has no more power of inventing a new value than of imagining a new primary colour, or, indeed, of creating a new sun and a new sky for it to move in."[32] Thus Satan's program of creating his own values in the mind's own place inevitably fails even in its greatest success: in spite of itself, it is forced to give ironic witness to the reality and validity of the *Tao*. The "brain of this foolish-compounded clay, man, is not able to invent anything," as Falstaff might say, of which this is not so.

If the *Tao* is indeed an inescapable reality, then the conception of human nature it calls for is upheld. "In the *Tao* itself, as long as we remain within it, we find the concrete reality in which to participate is to be truly human."[33] We are then beings who are driven to act, not just out of instinct, but on principle; that is, we are beings who have what Chesterton called a "mind." We find those principles to be part of a unified, objective reality over and above us as well as in us, which Lewis called the *Tao*. This *Tao* is not reducible to atoms in motion (and therefore neither are we). Though we find ourselves accountable to the *Tao*, we also rebel against it; and (though Lewis develops this part in other books) the best explanation of these realities is the doctrine that we are incarnated spirits made in the image of the one Spirit who was himself incarnate, embodied spirits who rebelled against him at the biblical fall and who can be redeemed by him even now. For what Lewis calls the *Tao* must therefore be absolute precisely because it is rooted in that Spirit's character as it is imprinted on his creation in general and as it is imaged in us, personal beings created in his image, in particular.

Its Implications for Politics

As we have seen, our view of man has ramifications for every area of life and thought. It might be useful here to notice that it is relevant not only for ethics, education, and religion but also for politics.[34] If Lewis' analysis of man's nature in relation to the *Tao* is correct, then it is possible to view human beings as having been "endowed by their Creator with certain inalienable rights." But the language of the American Declaration of Independence makes sense only on the basis of the doctrine of Creation. If God did not endow us with rights that correspond with the *Tao*-oriented nature he gave us when he made us, where do they come from? The only alternative is that they are sociological constructions created by the community as expressed in the state. Harold O. J. Brown puts the question very well: "Can we make whatever laws we please, or are we bound to respect a higher order in human affairs?"[35] The bottom line is that what the state giveth, the state can take away; sociologically generated rights by definition cannot be *inalienable*. Our only protection from this possibility would be if rights were grounded in something larger and more basic than the state or even than nature. As the founding fathers understood, the only way rights *can* be "inalienable" is if they are endowed by the Creator.

Hence Lewis is concerned in this book about the radical ways in which the new secular reductionist view of man erodes traditional barriers to tyranny. When we come to see ourselves merely as part of nature, like the other animals, we come to see the human race as something over which to extend our control, as we seek to do with the rest of nature. But the reality is that "what we call Man's power over Nature turns out to be a power exercised by some men over other men with Nature as its instrument."[36] And when there is no longer any distinction between man and nature, where is the limitation to that power?

If rights are no longer inalienable except in name, if traditional morality is dismissed as the unscientific and arbitrary imposition of rules by those dead white European males who held hegemony in the past in order to protect their own interests, and if the state wields the power of science unchecked by the *Tao* (i.e., traditional morality), then the possibilities are frightening indeed. "The final stage is come when Man by eugenics, by pre-natal conditioning, and by an education and propaganda based on a perfect applied psychology, has obtained full control over himself. *Human* nature will be the last part of Nature to surrender to Man."[37] But, then, who controls the controllers? "The last men, far from being the heirs of power, will be of all men most subject to the dead hand of the great planners and conditioners and will themselves exercise least power upon the future."[38] And those who are in control then will be as gods who are themselves ironically powerless to be anything more than demons: "At the moment, then, of Man's victory over Nature, we find the whole human race subjected to some individual men, and those individuals subjected to that in themselves which is purely 'natural'—to their irrational impulses. Nature, untrammeled by values, rules the Conditioners and, through them, all humanity. Man's conquest of Nature turns out, in the moment of its consummation, to be Nature's conquest of Man."[39]

If we reduce man to an animal or to a machine, thus ignoring our spiritual accountability to the *Tao*, then we must not expect ideals like democracy, equality, or justice to be more than words, arbitrary sounds floating in the air. As Gordon Lewis perceptively notes, "Postmodern thinkers cannot on Monday destroy belief in the universality and necessity of the laws of logic and morality and expect us to protect their human rights on Tuesday."[40] If this process is ever completed, then truly we must live either in Hobbes' "state of nature" where each person is subject to the predations of his neighbors and life is "solitary, nasty, poor, brutish, and short," or in Orwell's dystopia where it is subject to the manipulations of Big Brother and is collective, sanitized, physically comfortable, controlled, long, and meaningless. Or perhaps we will find a way to combine both in one horrible brave new world. The continued "progress" we have made toward those ends makes Packer probably right in saying that "were Lewis with us today, he would weep, I think, at the progress subjectivism has made in the last half-century," which includes an "indifference to truth that calls itself tolerance, and is enforced under the name of political correctness" and "the prevalence in educational circles of the deconstructionist dogma that human discourse never conveys public truth, but is only a power play."[41] Such is the unavoidable price of denying the *Tao* and with it the view of human nature which makes us able to respond to it. "It is like the famous Irishman who found that a certain kind of stove reduced his fuel bill by half and thence concluded that two stoves of the same kind would enable him to warm his house with no fuel at all. It is the magician's bargain: give up our soul, get power in return. But once our souls, that is, our selves, have been given up, the power thus conferred will not belong to us."[42]

Lewis's conclusions are inescapable. Either we find our humanity in the *Tao*, or we lose it. As Chesterton put it, a man is free to think of himself as a poached egg. But "if he is a poached egg, he is not free to eat, drink, sleep, walk, or smoke a cigarette." Likewise, he is free to think of himself as nothing more than atoms in motion, to accept secularism and materialism as the ultimate truth about himself. But then he is not logically free while doing so to "curse, to thank, to justify, to urge, to punish, to resist temptations, to incite mobs, to make New Year resolutions, to pardon sinners, to rebuke tyrants, or even to say 'thank you' for the mustard."[43] He is not logically free, as a secularist and materialist, to be *human*. Either objective value exists, and we can know it because it is grounded in the mind of the same

God who made our minds; or ideals like freedom, human rights, and justice are mere illusions. These affirmations all hang together; they logically entail one another. Therefore, to deny any part of this is indeed to attempt to abolish humanity itself.

Interlude

PROPOSED, THAT THE MODERN SCIENTIFIC WORLDVIEW, IN ITS EUPHORIA OVER LEARNING HOW TO DO NEAT THINGS WITH MATTER, HAS LEFT SOMETHING OUT OF THE EQUATION

Sonnets LVII–LVIII

There was a time when men could see the sky,
  A grand cathedral vaulted and ablaze
  With myriad candles lifted up on high
  By nights for vespers; in the brighter days,
The great rose window eastward shed its rays
  For morning prayer, and each and every flame
  Burned elegant in litanies of praise,
  In fugues and canons to extol the Name.
But now the sky, though larger, is more tame,
  And modern man sees what he's taught to see:
  Huge numbers are just numbers all the same,
  Though multiplied toward infinity;
And quarks and quasars cannot speak to us
  Except as agitated forms of dust.

Except as agitated forms of dust,
  We don't know how to know the thing we are:
  The biochemistry of love is lust
  As an atomic furnace is a star,
And all that's known is particles at war.
  And yet we do know love, and yet we know
  That it and lust are infinitely far
Apart. We know the stars and how they glow,
Though they know nothing of us here below.
  So, even while we're slogging through the mire,
  We cannot help ourselves, but as we go,
  We cock our heads to listen for the choir.
We know that half the truth is half a lie:
  There was a time when men could see the sky.
                                          —*D.T.W.*

Chapter Three

J. R. R. TOLKIEN: HUMANITY AND FAERIE

"The lunatic, the lover, and the poet
Are of imagination all compact. . . .
The poet's eye, in a fine frenzy rolling,
Doth glance from heaven to earth,
from earth to heaven,
And as imagination bodies forth
The forms of things unknown, the poet's pen
Turns them to shapes, and gives to airy nothing
A local habitation and a name."

—DUKE THESEUS, IN SHAKESPEARE'S
A MIDSUMMER NIGHT'S DREAM

LEWIS'S FRIEND J. R. R. TOLKIEN fought the abolition of man not only by writing an unbovine history of Middle Earth but also by thinking profoundly about the nature and significance of certain kinds of stories that our strange species has made and keeps coming back to. His essay "On Faerie Stories" is full of insight not only into the stories themselves but also their human makers and readers.

He finds them as creative as Chesterton did and participating in a Lewisian *Tao*, for they are compelled to make stories full of magic and marvels, stories in which good confronts evil and in which "keeping promises (even those with intolerable consequences)" forms "one of the notes of the horns of Elfland, and not a dim note."[1] But Tolkien goes on to be more explicit about where these myth-making qualities in our race come from, nailing down things that Chesterton and Lewis (in the books we have studied so far) only hinted at.

Creation and Subcreation

He does this by answering a friend who had questioned the value of myth for "enlightened" moderns.

> *"Dear Sir,"* I said—*"Although now long estranged,*
> *Man is not wholly lost nor wholly changed.*
> *Dis-graced he may be, yet is not de-throned.*
> *and keeps the rags of lordship once he owned:*
> *Man, Sub-creator, the refracted Light*
> *through whom is splintered from a single White*
> *to many hues, and endlessly combined*
> *in living shapes that move from mind to mind.*
> *Though all the crannies of the world we filled*
> *with Elves and Goblins, though we dared to build*
> *Gods and their houses out of dark and light,*
> *and sowed the seed of dragons—'twas our right*
> *(used or misused). That right has not decayed:*
> *we make still by the law in which we're made."*[2]

"We make still by the law in which we're made." I can still remember the excitement with which I first read those words as a young high-school student wrestling with whether I could still believe the Christian faith in which I had been reared, given the failure (actually, to be more honest, refusal) of the Christians

I knew to interact intelligently and responsibly with the problems of modern thought.[3] For Tolkien had just roped all the problems and their answers together in a single sentence. Man, in other words, is inexplicable by materialist reductionism because of the *imago Dei*; we love to tell and hear stories because we are made in the image of the Creator whose creation is in fact the story we call "History and Redemption." Or in terms more in keeping with Tolkien's defense of faerie, the human race is incapable of being fully explained or portrayed by either philosophical or literary naturalism. We are such irrepressible inventors and expressers of ourselves because we are made in the image of the Creator.[4] Hence our outlandish notions like riding horses, our many styles of nest adorned with unnecessary arts, and our addiction to ideals like rights, goodness, truth, and beauty, which refuse to be treated as mere subjective constructs no matter how hard our secular philosophies push us to do so.

But out of all these creative and *Tao*-inspired possibilities, Tolkien focuses on stories. He builds on the theology of literature found in Sidney's "Defense of Poesy," expanding it to meet modern questions and providing it with a critical vocabulary.[5] Every writer, like God, creates a world, determines the laws of its nature, and peoples it with characters whose significant actions give that world its meaning. God's "primary world" is reflected in our "secondary worlds," which, far from being mere escape or wish fulfillment, reflect back into the primary world the marvelous quality—the "enchantment"—that is really there by virtue of its created, its nonreductionist character, but which familiarity and secularist philosophy work to obscure.

Creation and Irreducibility

The idea of the world's (and man's) *createdness* as the explanation of their stubborn resistance to reductionism is an implication of Tolkien's analysis that is worth pondering for a moment. Its corollary is that the denial of the doctrine of creation is the explanation of our inability to resist the various futile flirtations with reductionism to which the modern world tempts us.

One could say of a story or a chapter that it is just marks on paper. One could support this conclusion by minute study of the chemical and spectrographic properties of the object in question, buttressed by so many footnotes that it began to look like a proof. But no matter how impressive, this analysis will never be accepted as complete by anyone who has read the words and found inspiration or a message worth receiving there. Now contrast the story with a piece of paper on which ink has been spilled. That object *is* reducible to marks on paper. The difference between the two is precisely the action of a creator. As a result of the absence or presence of such action, one object is an accident, the other an artifact. If we insist on treating the artifact as an accident, if we refuse to recognize any distinction between accidents and artifacts as even potentially valid because we have denied the possibility of a creator, we will never be able to understand the story. So we see that one who does not believe in creators (and hence in artifacts) is forced to be a reductionist, to treat and understand the story as if it were only an accidental and hence arbitrary inkblot. (Ironically, even our efforts to interpret that inkblot anyway as a kind of Rorschach test depend on the creativity that is shown by the storyteller, used in this case by the interpreter.) If our worldview precludes the possibility of a Creator, it must therefore preclude creators as well. And this is exactly the approach that secular thought is perforce committed to by its nature.

The story has a real, nonarbitrary meaning that goes beyond its physical properties because the act of creation ties it to something bigger than it is—the author, who has poured something, but not all, of his own plenitude of being into it. As Milton put it in *Areopagetica*, "Books are not absolutely dead things, but do contain a potency of life in them to be as active as that soul whose progeny they are; nay, they do contain, as in a vial, the purest efficacy and extraction of that living intellect that bred them."[6] Because he is created in the image of the infinite and eternal and therefore irreducible Creator, man is himself irreducible and gives some of this quality to his work. The paper with the ink spilled on it, on the other hand, is not related to anything other than a series of physical events. If we find a meaning in its ink, like the *Peanuts* characters seeing pictures in the clouds ("I see Beethoven composing the Fifth Symphony." "I see Napoleon fighting the Battle of Waterloo." "What do you see, Charlie Brown?" "I was going to say I saw a ducky and a horsy, but I changed my mind."), that meaning is necessarily arbitrary. But the meaning of the story is not arbitrary because there is something larger—the personality of the creator—behind it.

So Tolkien is saying that human beings themselves are like the story, not the inkblot. Human beings are creatures who can write irreducible stories (either on paper or in the medium of their lives) because they derive their own irreducibility from the Creator. In Tolkien's language they make because they are made.

The reductionism which is entailed in the nature of secular thought manifests itself in many ways in literary scholarship. Gaius and Titius in Lewis's *Green Book* reduced statements of value to statements of subjective emotion, thus reducing literature to the expression of subjective feelings. Postmodern deconstructionists reduce stories to arbitrary linguistic signs on paper in a way uncannily reminiscent of our story-versus-inkblot analogy, thus reducing literature to a branch of philosophy—skeptical epistemology—or to a branch of politics—leftist ideology. In a prophetic passage, Richard Weaver said that "certainly one of the most important revelations about a period comes in its theory of language, for that informs us whether language is viewed as a bridge to the noumenal or as a body of fictions convenient for grappling with transitory phenomena"[7]—an uncanny description of Deconstruction four decades before its arrival. Other postmodern scholars reduce truth to power and everything in history to race, class, and gender, thus reducing literature to a form of class warfare with white males as the enemy. Packer therefore remarks with real perspicacity: "That the shadows of French existentialism, Marxist atheism, and American hippiedom hang heavy over postmodernism, that reductionism rules its head while cynicism eats at its heart, and that its idea of political correctness makes it tyrannical towards dissentients much sooner than was ever the case with modernism itself are surely evident facts, and very disturbing facts too. Claiming to be a bracing disinfectant for the modern mind, postmodernism appears as a mode of intellectual anarchy, and in cultural terms as very much a dead-end street."[8] In Tolkien's day, stories were reduced to archaeology, compilations of sources, folklore, or mines of information for historical linguistics.

All these approaches are not without a certain kind of limited validity, for the story is also ink marks on paper; it is more, not less. But in so far as the secular cast of the modern mind is forced to absolutize such approaches and push them toward reductionism, they are dehumanizing and hence inhumane, leaving much that is significant out of consideration. They have "just the quality of the madman's argument: we have at once the sense of it covering everything and the sense of it leaving everything out of the picture."[9] That is why John Gardner was simply right when he said, "Every chance composition backs a lie. . . . Every nonsense artist, deconstructionist . . . is a plague carrier, a usurper of space that belongs to the sons of God."[10]

In his famous and seminal essay, *"Beowulf: The Monsters and the Critics,"* Tolkien gave us an allegory that is just as applicable to the modern forms of literary reductionism as it was to the ones he was trying to shake off in the 1930s. It deserves to be quoted in full:

A man inherited a field in which was an accumulation of old stone, part of an older hall. Of the old stone some had already been used in building the house in which he actually lived, not far from the old house of his fathers. Of the rest he took some and built a tower. But his friends coming perceived at once (without troubling to climb the steps) that these stones had formerly belonged to a more ancient building. So they pushed the tower over, with no little labour, in order to look for hidden carvings and inscriptions, or to discover whence the man's distant forefathers had obtained their building material. Some suspected a deposit of coal under the soil and began to dig for it, and forgot even the stones. They all said: "This tower is most interesting." But they also said (after pushing it over): "What a muddle it is in!" And even the man's own descendants, who might have been expected to consider what he had been about, were heard to murmur: "He is such an odd fellow! Imagine his using these old stones just to build a nonsensical tower! Why did he not restore the old house? He had no sense of proportion." But from the top of that tower, the man had been able to look out upon the sea.[11]

The Philosophy of Stories Revisited

Man then is that creature who can (even must) write stories; stories are artifacts irreducible to accidents; and they get that irreducibility from their creators, who got it from the Creator. Those stories tell us an awful lot about their creators, and their irreducibility to inkblots or atoms in motion is just the first of many things they show us. What Tolkien says is applicable to all stories but is most clearly evident in the kind he is actually writing about: fairy stories. He chose the fairy story because, like his own fiction, it "exists on the edges of the literary canon; it ignores or denies value to the empirical precepts of our culture; it defies the pragmatic morality and philosophy on which our culture rests; it is turned to, though often sheepishly or covertly, by a huge readership—hungry for something, not knowing what they seek."[12] Tolkien would go far toward explaining just what it is that we seek.

One feature of the fairy story which is central to Tolkien's literary apologetic is the happy ending. It is, he concludes, essential to the form, which begins "once upon a time" and ends "happily ever after." But it is not just the fact that things turn out well: "It is a sudden and miraculous grace. . . . It does not deny the existence of . . . sorrow and failure: the possibility of these is necessary to the joy of deliverance."[13] That is why, when the "turn" comes, there is "a catch of the breath, a beat and lifting of the heart . . . as keen as that given by any form of literary art."[14] To this moment he gives the technical name *eucatastrophe*.

Tolkien suggests that this moment of *eucatastrophe* in a well-constructed fairy story moves us so because it carries a glimpse of deeper realities about who we are—about our own story, as it were. As he explained to his son Christopher, "It produces its peculiar effect because it is a sudden glimpse of Truth; your whole nature chained in material cause and effect, the chain of death, feels a sudden relief as if a major limb out of joint had suddenly snapped back."[15] (If there is a Creator, his story is the Father of all stories—which is to say that there *is* one valid metanarrative, and postmodernists would not even have the ability to deny it if it did not exist.) And just as he made explicit what Chesterton had been hinting at when he appealed to the role of the *imago Dei* in our making or beginning, so here he is not reticent about spelling out the theological meaning of the climax of our larger story either: "God redeemed the corrupt making creatures, men, in a way fitting to this aspect, as to others, of their strange nature. The Gospels contain a fairy-story, or a story of a larger kind which embraces the essence of fairy-stories. . . . Among the marvels is the greatest and most complete conceivable *eucatastrophe*. But this story has entered History and the primary world."[16]

In other words, "man the story-teller would have to be redeemed in a manner consonant with his nature: by a moving story," which was also history and reality.[17] The incarnation, sacrifice, and resurrection of Christ not only complete and fulfill Old Testament prophecy; they also complete and fulfill the plots of all the great myths and fairy stories of the human race.

Tolkien's friend C. S. Lewis would develop this idea in *Miracles*. When Jesus turned the water into wine, he fulfilled the hints from nature that pagans had reified into Bacchus. When he multiplied the loaves, he fulfilled the hints that had led them to worship Ceres. "He is like the corn-king because the corn-king is a portrait of Him. The similarity is not in the least unreal or accidental. For the corn-king is derived (through human imagination) from the facts of Nature, and the facts of Nature from her Creator; the Death and Re-birth pattern is in her because it was first in Him."[18]

The death and resurrection of Christ is the fulfillment of much more than just Old Testament prophecy. All the hints in our literature that we are more than mere collocations of atoms coalesce into a coherent explanation of who and what we are when we see that this *eucatastrophe* is indeed the happy ending we were made for: fairy stories do capture something essential to a full view of reality. As Chesterton put it, "Fairyland is nothing but the sunny country of common sense."[19] Because of our creation in the image of God, we transcend the merely natural and cannot be reduced to atoms in motion. "*Supernatural* is a dangerous and difficult word in any of its senses, looser or stricter. But to fairies it can hardly be applied, unless *super* is taken merely as a superlative prefix. For it is man who is, in contrast to fairies, supernatural (and often of diminutive stature); whereas they are natural, far more natural than he. Such is their doom."[20]

We were made for a higher bliss, and we show it by our own making. We make because we were made in the image of the Maker.

What we make is sometimes corrupted because we fell from his grace. Chesterton put it this way: "God had written, not so much a poem, but rather a play; a play he had planned as perfect, but which has necessarily been left to human actors and stage managers who have since made rather a mess of it."[21] But the stories we make as we strut and fret our hour upon that stage still speak of our longing for restoration because we were made in the image of the Maker who is Savior and Redeemer as well. And Christ is what we have always been looking for. He is the ultimate definition of true humanity. So the one vantage point from which our whole strange and unbovine history makes sense is also the one place where myth and history are one: the spot where, in the light of the rising sun, the shadow of a cross points to the open door of an empty tomb.

A Parable for Demythologizers

"We come with rusty hatchets to chop down
Old Yggdrasil, the mightiest of trees;
We come with buckets full of air to drown
Old Triton, ruler of the seven seas.

For we are modern men, the heirs of time,
And won't be ruled by anything that's gone
Before. So if we think it more sublime
To exorcise Aurora from the dawn,

Then who is there who dares to say us nay?"
And so the desert wind swept through their minds
And found no obstacle placed in its way
To stop the stinging dust, the sand that blinds.

Blistered, parched, and withered, one by one
They fell beneath the branches of the tree,
Succumbing to the unrelenting sun
In cool green shade beside the roaring sea.

—D.T.W.

Chapter Four

THE ABOLITION OF HNAU

Perspectives on the Human in
The Space Trilogy

"But we are spirits of another sort."

—OBERON, IN SHAKESPEARE'S
A MIDSUMMER NIGHT'S DREAM

LEWIS'S *TAO* IS BY DEFINITION not an individual, nor even a human, nor even a merely terran phenomenon: it is truly *universal*, stamped by the Creator whose mind it reflects on the whole cosmos, or universe. But since we have perceived it mainly through the human conscience, the human mind, and human traditions, it is easy for us to be so close to it that we can miss it. But what if we could meet another animal species which also had a rational/spiritual nature and discover that, while separated from it by genetics, we were united with its mind in the *Tao*? That would be a truly instructive encounter. It would confirm the reality, the objectivity, and the universality of the *Tao* as we saw it in an unfamiliar setting. The similarities and the contrasts between ourselves and the other species would throw into

53

sharp relief both the nature of rational/spiritual animals in general and the uniqueness of our own way of incarnating that reality.

Whether reality holds such an encounter for us remains to be seen. But Lewis has imagined it for us in ways that are consistent with his explanation of the *Tao* in *The Abolition of Man*, and which therefore constitute a most interesting commentary on those ideas. The first work in which he did so is called The Space Trilogy: *Out of the Silent Planet, Perelandra,* and *That Hideous Strength.*

Often classed as science fiction, these books are in many ways really more like fantasy. The theory behind the technology in *Out of the Silent Planet* is vague and the knowledge of the solar system not even compatible with that available at the time.[1] Yet while science and technology do not function almost as characters, as was typical of the science fiction of the time, scientism does. The technology is both a means of visiting other worlds and a reminder that a certain philosophy of science is one of the major protagonists in the development of the plot, beginning with Weston's motives for space exploration in *Out of the Silent Planet* and culminating in the role of the National Institute for Coordinated Experiments, the "N.I.C.E.," in *That Hideous Strength.*

Out of the Silent Planet

While on a walking tour, philologist Elwin Ransom is kidnapped by the physicist Weston and his financier Devine. They have built a spaceship and traveled to the planet Malacandra (Mars), which they wish to exploit for its minerals, especially gold. Malacandra is now mostly barren *harandra,* but in the deep recesses of the *handramit* (canals), an atmosphere and a biosphere survive. On their previous trip Weston and Devine had misunderstood the seemingly primitive inhabitants to say that they could not return without bringing a human sacrifice for what they take to be a higher, ruling race, the

Sorns. When Ransom blunders into their lab, they realize that the disappearance of an academic on a long holiday will be much less suspicious than that of the servant boy they had planned to use, so they unwittingly transport a Christian linguist to this strange and new (to them) world.

When they get to Malacandra, Ransom discovers their plot and escapes. He is befriended by the hrossa, a nontechnological but intelligent otterlike species, learns their language, and lives in their society. Trying to explain the nature and history of the hmanna (men) to them is both embarrassing and enlightening, for they appear to be an unfallen race with no understanding of basic human emotions or motivations such as greed or selfishness. Later Ransom meets other races, the seroni (sorns), pfiffltriggi, and Oyarsa, the spiritual being (eldil) who rules over the entire planet. All of them worship Maleldil (etymologically "Great Spirit" in Old Solar) the Young, who has apparently had strange dealings with Ransom's quarantined world, Thulcandra ("the Silent Planet"), which they do not fully understand.

Together, pooling their knowledge, Ransom and Oyarsa come to a fuller understanding of humanity's "bentness" in thralldom to "The Bent One," the Oyarsa of Thulcandra, and of Maleldil's work for their redemption in spite of all. Weston and Devine are summoned to judgment before Oyarsa. But good materialist reductionists that they are, since they cannot see him, they assume his voice is some kind of a trick. It is hard to determine which is more deflating to their rationalistic humanism, their own behavior or Ransom's irreverently accurate translations of their pompous speeches in the dialogue with Oyarsa. They are banned from Malacandra and sent home with their vessel rigged to "unbody" once it reaches Earth. As a result of these adventures, Ransom comes to understand much about the true nature of man and the true spiritual nature of the universe. Weston and Devine go on to plot further mischief in future books, and Ransom begins to develop a network of like-minded people to oppose them.

Weston, the more philosophical-minded of the two villains, represents and is an eloquent mouthpiece for the kind of reductionistic materialism Lewis opposed in *The Abolition of Man*. He is full of high-minded idealism but has utterly rejected traditional morality as an unscientific impediment to the "progress" of the human race. Progress for whom, toward what, and at what expense are questions the reader is encouraged to ask.

As long as we root our understanding of human nature in the Christian doctrine of creation in the image of God, we are forced to a recognition of the sanctity of the individual and the need to find the right balance between the interests of the individual and the collective, the concrete person and the race as a whole. For creation applies not just to the race but to each individual. Each individual was made by God, is known by God (down to the hairs of one's head), matters to God, is destined to be saved or will be judged by God. Therefore the Christian worldview imposes limits on the subordination of the individual to the collective, needed to counteract the fact that the collective, being bigger, is inevitably stronger. That is why the individual has certain rights that cannot be abridged by the larger community no matter how strong the interests of the group. This is part of the basis for "inalienable" rights.

But if we move from this foundation to an evolutionary model as our basic paradigm for understanding man, it becomes difficult to find an unassailable place of protection for the individual against the collective. For evolution does not really apply to the individual organism but rather to the gene pool of the population as a whole; that is what adapts and changes. Those adaptations that contribute to greater survival value for the species are the ones which are preserved. The individual's only function is to try to pass his genes on to the next generation and to succeed or fail as a statistical average that changes the relative makeup of the gene pool over time. This is one reason it is so easy for the zealous adherents of materialist ideologies, whether of the left or of the right, to sacrifice the rights (and the lives) of individuals for the sake of a perceived improvement for the race (or nation, or interest group) as a whole. I am not suggesting that they have thought it through in these terms but simply that their worldview has no such built-in impediments to these rationalizations of evil as the Judaeo-Christian worldview does.

Weston then thinks very consistently with his own secular and materialist presuppositions. His justification for his intention of sacrificing the boy is an example: "'The boy was ideal,' said Weston sulkily. 'Incapable of serving humanity and only too likely to propagate idiocy. He was the sort of boy who in a civilized community would be automatically handed over to a state laboratory for experimental purposes.'"[2] Because the boy is retarded, he has no contribution to make that an intellectual like Weston can recognize. In terms of the later "sanctity of life" debate of our own times, we might say that the "quality of life" the retarded boy is capable of does not justify his continued existence over against the good (enhancement of quality of life) he could do the race by dying. Thus we can subtly cast in terms that sound like concern for the boy himself a justification for our use of him that is really purely selfish and utilitarian. We have not gotten to the point at which we would be comfortable sacrificing or experimenting on a child with, say, Down syndrome. But we are capable of sacrificing her to the perceived good of society, or to a perceived enhancement of the quality of life of her mother, by aborting her. We are also capable of experimenting on her while she is still a blastula, a ball of cells that does not particularly look like us but is capable of producing stem cells we think we can use. The triumph of Weston's secular worldview and its concept of humanity makes continued steps down this path inevitable.

Ransom and Weston get into a debate over the propriety of Weston's actions in which the implications of Weston's view of human nature become plain. Weston says, "We have learned how to jump off the speck of matter on which our species began; infinity, and therefore perhaps eternity, is being put into the hands of the human race. You cannot be so small-minded as to think that the rights or the life of an individual or of a million individuals are of the slightest importance in comparison with this."[3] But Ransom ignores Weston's attempted use of the fallacy of poisoning the well ("You cannot be so small-minded . . .") and does disagree, beginning to fulfill a role he will make a career of before the book is over: that of translating Weston's rhetoric into plain terms that reveal the true evil behind it. "I consider your philosophy of life raving lunacy. I suppose all that stuff about infinity and eternity means that you think you are justified in doing anything—absolutely anything—here and now, on the off chance that some creature or other descended from man as we know him may crawl about a few centuries longer in some part of the universe." But Weston, blinded by his pseudo-scientific materialism, is incapable of benefiting from this service. "'Yes—anything whatever,' returned the scientist sternly."[4] Thus he and his contemporary descendants illustrate Lewis's point in *Abolition* that when man subsumes himself under a materialist science, he actually loses the power of self-determination. For if any given individual is worthless and can be sacrificed to the perceived good of the whole, then what is the value of the continuation of the species? Weston is ironically acting out of the pure instinct that drives any species to try to survive. There is nothing uniquely human left for him to try to preserve.

Much of the most fascinating insight into human nature comes from Ransom's encounters with other species who are *hnau*, rational/spiritual animals like man but, in the case of the Malacandrian races, unfallen. Getting used to the whole idea of another rational animal is itself an eye-opening experience. We are so used to ourselves being both animal and rational that the strangeness of our own species, as Chesterton noted, is easy to miss. But when through Lewis's imagination we encounter those same features in something that does not look like us, the result is like Chesterton's strange bird who, by sticking statues of famous birds in front of his nest, became a fearful wildfowl indeed. So Ransom has moments when Hyoi's strangeness (which, if we have absorbed *The Everlasting Man,* we realize is also our own) suddenly hits home.

> It was only many days later that Ransom discovered how
> to deal with these sudden losses of confidence. They arose
> when the rationality of the *hross* tempted you to think of it
> as a man. Then it became abominable—a man seven feet
> high, with a snaky body, covered, face and all, with thick
> black animal hair, and whiskered like a cat. But starting
> from the other end you had an animal with everything an
> animal ought to have—glossy coat, liquid eye, sweet breath
> and whitest teeth—and added to all these, as though
> Paradise had never been lost and earliest dreams were true,
> the charm of speech and reason. Nothing could be more
> disgusting than the one impression; nothing more delight-
> ful than the other. It all depended on the point of view.[5]

We realize of course that man is just as strange and wonderful a creature to hross as hross is to man.

The hrossa naturally are extremely curious about their new friend. But in trying to answer their questions, Ransom begins to realize that the differences between man and hross go beyond body type and are in fact as significant as the similarities. He first notices this in the unexpected difficulties he finds in explaining Earth to them. They are amazed at how much the hmana are concerned with the problems of lifting and carrying things, reminding us of Richard Weaver's noting in *Ideas Have Consequences* that, with the world now "more than ever dominated by the gods of mass and speed," the "worship of these can lead only to the lowering of standards, the adulteration of quality, and, in general, to the loss of those things which are essential to the life of civility and culture."[6] But there are greater difficulties in explaining Earth to them even than this.

Naturally his conversations with the *hrossa* did not all turn on Malacandra. He had to repay them with information about Earth. He was hampered in this both by the humiliating discoveries which he was constantly making of his own ignorance about his native planet, and partly by his determination to conceal some of the truth. He did not want to tell them too much of our human wars and industrialisms. . . . A sensation akin to that of physical nakedness came over him whenever they questioned him too closely about men—the *hmana* as they called them. . . . What he did tell them fired the imagination of the *hrossa*: they all began making poems about the strange *handra* where the plants were hard like stone and the earth-weed green like rock and the waters cold and salt, and *hmana* lived out on top, on the *harandra*.[7]

Familiarity with ourselves blinds us not only to what is strange about us by design, our unique position in creation, but also to what is strange about us because it is abnormal. But the hrossa make us see all this again for the first time. For, as Ransom gradually begins to realize, they are unfallen. They are in some ways what we might have been had it not been for our rebellion against God. They cannot understand the motivations that cause the hmana to go to war or to be unfaithful to their mates. *Why would anyone want to live that way?* they wonder. The interconnectedness of human follies and their ultimate rootedness in the "bentness" of human nature become apparent in the hrossa's dialogues with Ransom. For human nature is bent away from Maleldil and toward a self-defeating selfishness. We justify the greed that leads to wars of conquest by scarcity of resources and overpopulation. But neither would be a problem if it were not for our sexual greed and incontinence. The hrossa are mystified by all of this. If someone needed food, why not give it to them? Why have more children than you can feed? "Isn't sex a pleasure?" Ransom asks. Oh, yes, a very great one. But that's no reason for its overindulgence. Why would a person want to eat after he was full or rest when he wasn't tired?

Ransom pondered this. Here, unless Hyoi was deceiving him, was a species naturally continent, naturally monogamous. And yet, was it so strange? Some animals, he knew, had regular breeding seasons; and if nature could perform the miracle of turning the sexual impulse outward at all, why could she not go further and fix it, not morally but instinctively, to a single object? He even remembered dimly having heard that some terrestrial animals, some of the "lower" animals, were naturally monogamous. Among the *hrossa*, anyway, it was obvious that unlimited breeding and promiscuity were as rare as the rarest perversions. At last it dawned upon him that it was not they, but his own species, that were the puzzle. That the *hrossa* should have such instincts was mildly surprising; but how came it that the instincts of the *hrossa* so closely resembled the unattained ideals of that far-divided species Man whose instincts were so deplorably different? What was the history of Man?[8]

Ransom will of course realize by the time he has met Oyarsa that the biblical doctrine of the Fall is the answer to his question. At this point Lewis wisely leaves it hanging unanswered for the reader to ponder. He is not preaching Christian doctrine as such but rather doing what is proper to fiction, creating an imaginative matrix within which the Christian doctrines that are the answer to man's mystery can make sense.

The hrossa seem to be a truly rational species, one whose reason has not been clouded (or "bent") by selfishness and greed. The fall then has compromised, but not destroyed, man's rationality; for Ransom is rational enough to understand the irrationality and the shame of his species. After all, as Chesterton reminds us, "Original sin [is] the only part of Christian doctrine which can really be proved."[9] Still, a bent hnau is not the same thing as a non-hnau; it is both better and worse. Ransom's life with the hrossa therefore heightens his sense of the need for redemption. Hence, when he participates in the hunt for the hnakra, his strong feeling that "whatever happened, he must show that the human species also were *hnau*."[10] Unfortunately, efforts to redeem oneself, even in one's own eyes (for the status of man as hnau is not an issue for anyone but him), tend to backfire, and Ransom's failure immediately to obey the eldil who had told him to go to Meldilorn leads to the death of his friend Hyoi at the hands of Weston and Devine.

"Hyoi, can you hear me?" said Ransom with his face close to the round seal-like head. "Hyoi, it is through me that this has happened. It is the other *hmana* who have hit you, the bent two that brought me to Malacandra. They can throw death at a distance with a thing they have made. I should have told you. We are all a bent race. We have come here to bring evil on Malacandra. We are only half *hnau*—Hyoi . . ." His speech died away into the inarticulate. He did not know the words for "forgive," or "shame," or "fault," hardly the word for "sorry." He could only stare into Hyoi's distorted face in speechless guilt. But the *hross* seemed to understand. It was trying to say something, and Ransom laid his ear close to the working mouth. Hyoi's dulling eyes were fixed on his own, but the expression of a *hross* was not even now perfectly intelligible to him.

"*Hma—hma*," it muttered and then at last "*Hman, hnakra-punt.*" Then there came a contortion of the whole body, a gush of blood and saliva from the mouth; his arms gave way under the sudden dead weight of the sagging head, and Hyoi's face became as alien and animal as it had seemed at their first meeting.[11]

This passage is full of interesting details that cry out for commentary. Man, it is suggested, is only "half hnau": he has compromised, but not erased completely, the spiritual nature Maleldil gave him at his creation. Lewis clearly rejected the doctrine of total depravity. It is also clear from his reasons for rejecting it that he did not understand it. He objects that "if our depravity were total we should not know ourselves to be depraved" and that experience observes much good in human nature.[12] Of course, these objections are beside the point. This common misunderstanding arises from confusing *total* depravity with *utter* depravity. According to one standard summary, total depravity does not imply that every sinner is "as thoroughly depraved as he can possibly become" or that there is no good in man; indeed, classical reformed thought affirms that there is much good in fallen human beings by common grace. Rather, the *total* means that the pollution of our nature by sin is totally "pervasive": "the inherent corruption extends to every part of man's nature, to all the faculties and powers of both soul and body."[13] As a result, though much natural good may remain by common grace,[14] we are totally unable (apart from special grace) to do anything that is spiritually good or worthy of salvation. It is not so clear that Lewis would have disagreed with this formulation of total depravity or that any of his human characters are an exception to it. So "half hnau" as a metaphorical description of what fallen humanity has made of itself is not one that classical Protestants need shy away from. The remnants of the *imago Dei* still distinguish us from the other animals but no longer unite us to God, apart from redemption.

There is nothing Ransom can do to repair the damage that fallen human nature has wrought. Even though he is only indirectly responsible for Hyoi's death—he was not the triggerman, he did not intend it, and it is only his neglect of the eldil's command that has contributed to it (but that was enough)—he is frozen in guilt and shame, powerless to extricate himself or move on. But then grace is extended by the victim of his inaction. With his last breath Hyoi names Ransom "Man, Hnakra-Slayer" because of his participation in the hunt. Ransom can find no Malacandrian words for guilt or forgiveness not just because he is still learning the language but perhaps because they do not exist. In an unfallen world they have (up until now) not been needed. Even Oyarsa must use the metaphor of "bentness" to speak of the humans' sinfulness. But Hyoi in a profoundly moving act finds a way of conveying forgiveness and grace ("unmerited favor") without the words: with his last breath he confers honor undeserved upon the guilt-ridden *hman* who kneels before him. Whatever Lewis's doctrinal understanding (or lack of it), he has given us a powerfully effective picture of the biblical teaching on sin and forgiveness, inability and grace.

Finally, Hyoi's death scene underscores the importance of the nonmaterial, *Tao*-oriented component of the hybrid physical/spiritual nature of all hnau, including man. When the spirit departs at the moment of death, the transformation of this face that Ransom and we have come to love is horrible: for that face, after all he and Ransom have been through together, to become "alien and animal" again is a hard lesson indeed. But it pictures the nonreducible nature of hnau. Hrossa, like humans, cannot be reduced to their physical form alone and still be what they were created to be. That is the horror of death: Hyoi is hnau no longer.

So Ransom finally sets out on his trip to Meldilorn to answer Oyarsa's summons. On the way he meets Augray the Sorn. There is a certain division of labor among the species on Malacandra: the hrossa tend to be the poets, the seroni are the philosophers and scientists, and the pfkeyltriggi are the craftsmen. Augray is able to explain more to Ransom about the history of the solar system and to show him a telescopic vision of Thulcandra, the Silent Planet ruled by the rebellious and evil Bent One. Those astronauts who have been able to look back on earth from space have tended to remark on its beauty and fragility. But if they had spent some months living with and getting to know an unfallen race, and then bringing harm to it, they might have had a different reaction. "It was all there in that little disk—London, Athens, Jerusalem, Shakespeare. There everyone had lived and everything had happened; and there presumably, his pack was still lying in the porch of an empty house near Sterk. 'Yes,' he said dully to the *sorn*. 'That is my world.' It was the bleakest moment in all his travels."[15] Learning to accept one's own bentness is the first step to being straightened. But it is not a pleasant experience, however necessary.

Ransom has spent a bit of time trying to understand the Malacandran races. Now the sorns return the favor, attempting to fathom why the human race, while undoubtedly hnau, is also so bent. Though they have not read the terran Scriptures, of course, their insight leads them to a remarkable echo of the terms of Satan's offer: ye shall be as gods.

"It is because they have no Oyarsa," said one of the pupils.

"It is because every one of them wants to be a little Oyarsa himself," said Augray.

"They cannot help it," said the old *sorn*. "There must be rule, yet how can creatures rule themselves? Beasts must be ruled by *hnau* and *hnau* by *eldila* and *eldila* by Maleldil. These creatures have no *eldila*. They are like one trying to lift himself by his own hair—or one trying to see

over a whole country when he is on a level with it—like a
female trying to beget young on herself."[16]
Though Oyarsa is not God but something analogous to an angel, he
represents God and rules for God (Maleldil) on Malacandra. So the
desire to be little Oyarsas is in effect the desire to be like God—not
just *knowing* good and evil (which man would undoubtedly have
learned in time without falling prey to evil if he had been obedi-
ent) but desiring like Milton's Satan to usurp God's prerogative of
determining good and evil in the mind's own place. ("Evil be thou
my good.")

We might learn the futility of this enterprise from our own daily
lives if we were not too close to them. The old sorn's similes can help
bring that truth into focus. They may also be relevant as explanations
of why our redemption, which must involve among other things
the "straightening" of this particular bentness, must be by grace.
Salvation by works is much like a female trying to beget the fruit of
the Spirit on herself. If indeed our first parents wanted to "call their
souls their own," to find some corner of the universe of which they
could say to God, "This is our business, not yours,"[17] which is what
the desire to be little Oyarsas involves, and if this is wrong because
it is a lie, then the pursuit of salvation by our own merit is doomed
because it is an attempted repudiation of the lie that reaffirms it
even as it purports to turn from it. One must start by giving up the
claim that your soul is yours, not even yours to save or lose. It is His,
period, and only by giving it back to him completely can we ever hope
to find it again. But he who gives up his life, the same shall find it.

Another of the sorn's comments sheds an interesting light on
fallen man's status as hnau, rational/spiritual animal. As hnau man
is rational, but as fallen he is only semirational. So the sorns are
struck by the fact that Thulcandra apparently has only one kind of
hnau. "Your thought must be at the mercy of your blood," said the
old *sorn*. "For you cannot compare it with thought that floats on

a different blood."[18] The implications of this observation include, first, the assumption that thought is not reducible to "blood," i.e., to a function of the physical organism. It can be influenced by hormones, temperament, etc., but it ultimately transcends these things. Contemporary thinkers like Lakoff and Johnson are suspicious of any concept of reason as "disembodied" because they assume that our only access to it is through minds that inhabit human bodies just like ours. They make many fascinating observations about how our use of metaphorical structures to construct and mediate our knowledge is related to our bodily existence. Unfortunately, they ultimately fail to avoid reducing all truth claims to mere anthropocentric perspectives.[19] But what if we could examine thought that floated on a different blood? We would either discover that there were no universal truths of reason that weren't species/perspective-dependent (in which case communication would be impossible, so how would we know we had encountered another mind?), or we would discover that there really are such universal truths of reason in spite of our bodily and cultural differences. But this would mean that something in reason transcends blood and that even through our blood we have access to truths that are not dependent on a particular form of embodiment.

Lewis's imagining such thought in hross or sorn does not make it real, but it does help us imaginatively to grasp one of the claims of Christian epistemology, which is that we do have access to an even more radical test case than this. What about thought that floats on no blood at all? The eternal *Logos* exists and is part of our minds through the fact that we were created in its image. The inescapable Tao and its toehold in our irreducible minds attest to this reality and give us a basis for appreciating the insights of scholars like Lakoff and Johnson without falling prey to the reductionism they have no way to avoid. The only epistemology that can successfully avoid the Kantian dilemma (that our bodies ultimately prevent us from ever having any direct knowledge of the *Ding an sich,* the thing in itself) depends on the anthropology that says we were created in the image of God. The Reason that structured our minds is the same One that designed and made the external world they have to deal with. Though our reason may not be disembodied (we will for sake of simplicity ignore the questions raised by the intermediate state our souls enjoy between death and the resurrection), it is tied to One that is. The fall distorts and clouds but does not obliterate that tie; our fall, not the absence of other hnau, is ultimately what puts our reason too often at the mercy of our blood. Fortunately, the old sorn could not have known this, so we get the benefit of his illuminating though in one sense erroneous theory.

The importance of the *imago Dei* for Lewis's (or any Christian) picture of human nature cannot be overestimated. It allows Ransom to communicate not only with other hnau but even with what would seem to us a disembodied spirit. (Lewis, like Milton, speculates that maybe angels have a kind of body; but in any case it is so radically different from ours that it makes the point just as well.) For, as Oyarsa reminds him, "We are both copies of Maleldil."[20] There is common ground that transcends common physical form, common environment, common genetics, for it is ultimately rooted in the Tao.

Applying the *imago* not only to other hnau but even to Oyarsa brings out a facet of the image easier to miss in, though equally true of, the individuals of our own species: to be an image is to be a portrait, not a clone. Each of the species brings one part of the Maker's character to the forefront while having common ground in the fact that these are facets of one unified Personality. Within a single species, like man, each individual does the same thing. The Tao is not a straitjacket but a form that allows for endless variety without chaos. It is the limiting condition that makes true freedom possible, the unity that provides the substratum from which alone true individuality can grow.

Weston's inability to understand these truths leaves him suscep-tible to many errors. He claims to be working for the sake of man, for man's ability to colonize and exploit other planets will help to ensure the survival of the human species. Yet Oyarsa cannot understand what it is that Weston actually loves about man. It is not the form of the human body, for Weston's evolutionary doctrine teaches him that the future descendants for whom he works may be unrecognizable. It is not any particular individual, for he is willing to sacrifice any number of them to achieve his goal. Nor is it man's mind, for then he would love mind wherever he found it. Finally, Oyarsa asks, "But if it is neither man's mind, which is as the mind of all other hnau—is not Maleldil maker of them all?—or his body, which will change—if you care for neither of these, what do you mean by man?"[21]

To this question Weston has no answer. Nor, indeed, can he, for he is an accurate (if exaggerated) embodiment of secularist reduc-tionism. Rejecting the Tao, he has stepped away from it toward the void, and he will fall into that void most horribly in the next book. Seeing this, Oyarsa banishes him from Malacandra forever and sends Ransom back with him to continue the battle in future install-ments. For this battle between light and darkness, good and evil, is unavoidably a battle between two rival conceptions of who man is: Weston's philosophy unchecked would be the abolition of man as hnau because, in its rejection of the Tao, it is simply the attempted abolition of hnau.

Perelandra

Ransom returns to Earth but does not cease to have dealings with eldila, who decide to send him to Perelandra (Venus) in order to deal with the fact that Weston has constructed a new spaceship and is planning to go there. Ransom is transported in a coffinlike box, lands in a Perelandran sea, pulls himself onto a floating island, and meets the Green Lady. It turns out that Perelandra is a newer world, and the Green Lady and her husband its Adam and Eve. Weston yields himself completely to the Bent One, who possesses him and tries through his body to tempt the Lady to disobey Maleldil by sleeping on the fixed land, i.e., on the continent rather than one of the floating islands—this being the prohibition in that world rather than the eating of a particular fruit. It falls to Ransom to try to oppose this attempt. At first he does so through reason. But the Unman (Weston's body used by the Bent One) is so unscrupulous in argument that Ransom eventually realizes that he is doomed to failure and hence has to destroy the Unman, the Bent One's instrument, by force. Perelandra is saved, and Ransom is returned to Thulcandra (Earth), where the forces that Weston and Devine have set in motion must be confronted in the next and final installment.

Until he wrote *'Til We Have Faces*, Lewis thought *Perelandra* his best book, and many of his readers have agreed. Though reason alone fails to deliver Perelandra from the threat, the conversations with the Lady and debates with the Unman are full of insight into the nature of temptation, the meaning of our own fall, and the basic philosophies of life that must characterize those who truly worship God and those who reject him, precisely because they flow from that acceptance or rejection. The book often rises to a truly mythic level with the contrast between the floating islands and the fixed land, for example, making a wonderful symbol for the unavoidable choice between insistence on determining our own future as opposed to accepting what Maleldil sends us on the next wave (or, to anticipate the diction of another series, "accepting the adventure Aslan sends us"). And for our purposes in this study, it presents us with a new set of foils to set off and reveal human nature.

Tor and Tinidril, the Adam and Eve of Perelandra, unlike the hnau of Malacandra, look (except for their color) human, but they are not. They do not share our ancestry, our genes, our history, or (most importantly) our fall. Thus they allow Lewis to pursue further and in new ways the theme broached on Malacandra that there is more to incarnate mind and personality, that is to hnau, than outward form. Neither the absence of that form on the part of the hrossa nor its presence on the part of the Green Lady have the implications one would expect on the basis of secular materialism. Tor and Tinidril show us what man once was and, after they have successfully resisted the temptation that tripped us, what we might have been. Then the Unman shows us something that once was human and still has the outward form but has lost the essence of humanity. He has ironically become what his philosophy by implication said he was, the mere puppet of the forces of created nature, though they turn out to be something much more sinister than merely the impersonal laws of physics and chemistry.

When Ransom first meets Tinidril, he is immediately aware of the difference: "Never had Ransom seen a face so calm, and so unearthly, despite the full humanity of every feature. He decided afterwards that the unearthly quality was due to the complete absence of that element of resignation which mixes, in however slight a degree, with all profound stillness in terrestrial faces. This was a calm which no storm had ever preceded. It might be idiocy, it might be immortality, it might be some condition of mind to which terrestrial experience offered no clue at all."[22]

Man in his present state is a creature who cannot know peace without resignation. We are a species of sorrow and acquainted with grief. Peace is for us an attainment, not a natural condition, therefore all the more to be admired and respected when found, for it never comes without a price. And that price in a fallen world is twofold. First, one must come to terms with the many unalterable things in one's circumstances which range from the annoying to the griev- ous. But even more difficult than that acceptance is the resigning of one's own will, the laying down of the arms of our rebellion, the

giving up of our aspirations to be little Oyarsas ourselves. There is
no true peace possible for us without these surrenders. And the face
of Tinidril brings this aspect of the human condition into poignantly
sharp focus. For hers is a peace bought at no such prices, therefore in
some ways deeper, in some ways less profound, in many ways alien to
anything we have ever known. But by it we know ourselves better.

Ransom had been prepared by his visit to Malacandra to see past
external appearance; he had discovered rational mind and friendship
under an alien exterior. Now he wonders if the opposite will happen:
will he find an alien intelligence in a familiar form? No. Tinidril is
also hnau. But she reinforces the lesson that the essence of humanity lies in something more profound than the body. Hyoi had to be
accepted as part of the community of hnau though not resembling
man; Tinidril, though hnau, must be accepted as not human even
though she does resemble us. And therein lies an interesting realization about what it means to be a part of the human community.
"Now he realized that the word 'human' refers to something more
than the bodily form or even to the rational mind. It refers also to
that community of blood and experience which unites all men and
women on the Earth. But this creature was not of his race; no wind-
ings, however intricate, of any genealogical tree, could ever establish
a connection between himself and her. In that sense, not one drop
in her veins was 'human.' The universe had produced her species and
his quite independently."[23]

Ransom had already noticed that meeting another species of
hnau meant not only dealing with individuals such as Hyoi but also
learning the similarities and differences between two societies. Now
Tinidril, though she is so far only an individual, in her own way brings
into focus what it means to be a part of the human race: humanity
is a community, a family bound by " blood and experience," that is
by a common nature, a common ancestry, and a common history.
Two people from opposite sides of the world may not be able to trace

their separate family histories to a common root, but it is there, and no human being's experience of life can be completely irrelevant to any other's, for all belong to the whole. As Donne says, "No man is an island entire of itself; every man is a piece of the continent. . . . If a clod be washed away by the sea, Europe is the less, as well as if a promontory were, as well as if a manor of thy friend's or of thine own were. Any man's death diminishes me, because I am involved in mankind."[24] The civilized Englishman and the remote tribesman have a common bond that is easy for them to miss if neither has met the Green Lady of Perelandra.

Ransom gets many opportunities to grow in his understanding of the human condition by seeing the contrast between what we are and what we might have been. One such opportunity is observing the relations between Tinidril and the Perelandran beasts. When she interacts with the animals, "It was not really like a woman making much of a horse, nor yet a child playing with a puppy. There was in her face an authority, in her caresses a condescension, which by taking seriously the inferiority of her adorers made them somehow less inferior—raised them from the status of pets to that of slaves."[25]

Lewis makes a rare mistake here, underestimating the difficulty many modern readers will have with the connotations of the word *slave*: it will be hard for many to see that as a "raising" in any sense. If we substitute the word *servant,* I think we will be able to see his point. The fall not only made us subject to mortality, but it also put our reason at the mercy of our blood. In other words, our rebellion was an attack on right order, on the benevolent hierarchy inherent in the relation of Creator to creature. The result was naturally a disruption of the lower levels of that hierarchy: our bodies rebel against our minds (reason at the mercy of blood), and the benevolent and paternal rule of the animal kingdom, of beast by hnau, that we were intended to exercise was also disordered. Now instead of tending the garden, we pollute it; instead of caring for the animals, we exploit them.

As in every other case, God has mercifully restrained this tendency to corruption we let loose into the world. As we have not become totally irrational, so we have not completely lost our proper relationship to nature as God's benevolent deputies or subregents. We pollute the environment, but we also set up national parks and wilderness areas. And we feel a need for affectionate relationships with those animals who are susceptible that sometimes seem to rise to friendship. Pets are a symptom of our estrangement from Eden and our longing to get back home. "Man with dog closes a gap in the universe."[26] And this can be good, but it is never, Ransom realizes, what it might have been. We can get back some of what we have lost, but it is never the same.

One of Lewis's goals in much of his writing is to rehabilitate the concept of hierarchy.[27] The universe, or any individual person or community within it, is in harmony when matter obeys soul and soul obeys reason, which reflects the mind of God. Or, to put it another way, beasts should obey hnau, hnau eldila, eldila their Oyarsa, and the oyeresu Maleldil, as Ransom learned in his visit to the sorns. This order is reflected on many levels in the divinely constituted order ("the powers that be") in the state, the church, and the family. The problem of course is that by rebelling against God, we have corrupted not only ourselves but also the order which he designed for the world. So the hierarchy that was intended to be harmonious and benevolent is too often actually experienced in a fallen world as hurtful and oppressive. This leads many modern (or postmodern) people to reject hierarchy itself as evil. But the problem is rather that it is a good thing corrupted. Just as we do not totally yield to irrationality because our reason is at the mercy of our blood, nor to exploitation and cruelty because we no longer live in Eden, so too, Lewis would argue, we must not abandon hierarchy because it has been corrupted but rather seek to restore it by God's grace so that it works properly again. One way of doing that is to create pictures of what such an order would look like. That is part of the function of our vision of Tinidril with the beasts.

We are not allowed to enjoy the Edenic vision too long, though. The Bent One through Weston begins the temptation of the Perelandran Eve with Ransom playing the role of "good angel." But the Unman seems to be operating at an unfair advantage. For him reason is not the divine guide to truth but a pragmatic tool to be used or discarded according to the needs of the moment. He is free to mix lies and half-truths in his presentations. Ransom cannot. And the Lady, with no experience that could enable her to spot lies or distinguish reason from rationalization, is at risk of being deceived. Ransom realizes with a jolt that he could well lose. "It was suddenly borne in upon him that her purity and peace were not, as they had seemed, things settled and inevitable like the purity and peace of an animal—that they were alive and therefore breakable, a balance maintained by a mind and therefore, at least in theory, able to be lost. There is no reason why a man on a smooth road should lose his balance on a bicycle; but he could. There was no reason why she should step out of her happiness into the psychology of our own race; but neither was there any wall between to prevent her doing so."28

Tinidril, like Eve, was "sufficient to have stood but free to fall."29 Readers familiar with Milton and other older writers will of course note that Lewis, the quintessential "Old Western Man,"30 seems original to modern readers because he is anything but; because he taps into a rich tradition of art and thought which has largely, to our detriment, been forgotten. What does it mean to be "sufficient to have stood but free to fall"? Here the adventure of being hnau—of operating with a mind that has to understand and decide, as opposed to operating by instinct—threatens to become much worse than one of those nasty, uncomfortable things that make you late for dinner.

The balance (another word for *harmony*) of Tinidril's world is a picture of what Augustine said life was like for our own Adam and

Eve before their fall. "They had been given the ordered equilibrium of all parts, the balance of appetite, the harmonious correspondence of conduct and conviction that brings internal peace."[31] But Tinidril's balance has to be maintained by her mind, just as theirs did; it is something she does, not simply something she enjoys. The doing is obedience, which is a conscious choice, and the whole purpose of the prohibition of the fixed land is to make that choice possible. It is to create an obedience that can be for the sake of obedience, for every other action Maleldil requires of her is something she would want to do anyway. The harmony of the Perelandran/Edenic order flows from that obedience, the proper response of the rational creature to its Creator. If she should stop doing it, the hierarchy and the harmony that flow from it would be destroyed not only as a judicial consequence but also by the nature of the act.

Ransom (Tinidril calls him "Piebald" because of the uneven sunburn he got while in suspended animation on his way from Earth) achieves one of his temporary victories when he explains this to her. Obedience is good and right and delightful for its own sake when walking with Maleldil; to accept the good he gives (being where the waves take one) rather than insisting on what one had anticipated (waking up at the same spot on the fixed land where one went to sleep) need not be a surrender or a sacrifice but a positive act of joy.

"And this, O Piebald, is the glory and wonder you have made me see; that it is I, I myself, who turn from the good expected to the given good. Out of my own heart I do it. One can conceive a heart which did not: which clung to the good it had first thought of and turned the good which was given it into no good. . . . I thought," she said, "that I was carried in the will of Him I love, but now I see that I walk with it. I thought that the good things He sent me drew me into them as the waves lift the islands; but now I see that it is I who plunge into them with my own legs and arms, as when we go swimming. I feel as if I were living in that roofless world of yours where men walk undefended beneath naked heaven. It is a delight with terror in it! One's own self to be walking from one good to another, walking beside Him as Himself may walk, not even holding hands. How has He made me so separate from Himself? How did it enter His mind to conceive such a thing? The world is so much larger than I thought."[32]

This is indeed a delight with a terror in it, the terror of the breakable balance. But the terror can be an excitement that enhances the joy rather than an omen of the danger of loss. It all depends on whether Tinidril keeps turning herself out of her own heart to the good which is Maleldil, whether she keeps on walking beside him. She is not human because she has never stopped doing this. We are because we have. But it is the same doing. And thus it is a picture not only of what we were like before the fall but also of the Christian life, the life to which we are in the process of being restored through redemption. The best of us in this life no longer walk thus so much as stumble. But we are learning. Watching the Lady's steady steps can help. And when Christ returns, we will be enabled to stride surely once again.

One way of understanding Ransom's humanity is to see him placed between the Lady and the Unman, the place he occupies literally in the debates which constitute her temptation. He occupies that place conceptually as well. She is humanity as it might have been and as Ransom when he is fully redeemed will be. Having never fallen, she is, in one sense, above us. But Weston is one who has willfully forfeited that arresting of our fall which by common grace preserves vestiges of goodness in all of us and which by special grace can restore even the worst of us to something that even now provides glimpses and adumbrations of the Lady's walking, foretastes of the day when the restoration will be complete. He has forfeited that arresting by deliberately calling the Bent One into himself, yielding himself fully to his power. And the Bent One has used him up and discarded him, leaving almost nothing left. If the Lady is in one sense superhuman, the Unman has become subhuman. But thus he also illustrates part of the human condition. We are creatures poised between these two opposing destinies, with all still in the balance. And that is to walk naked beneath the fiery heavens indeed. "The forces which had begun, perhaps years ago, to eat away his humanity had now completed their work. The intoxicated will which had been slowly poisoning the intelligence and the affections had now at last poisoned itself and the whole psychic organism had fallen to pieces. Only a ghost was left—an everlasting unrest, a crumbling, a ruin, an odour of decay. 'And this,' thought Ransom, 'might be my destination; or hers.'"[33]

Or, as Lewis put it elsewhere:

It is a serious thing to live in a society of possible gods
and goddesses, to remember that the dullest and most
uninteresting person you talk to may one day be a creature
which, if you saw it now, you would be strongly tempted
to worship, or else a horror and a corruption such as you
now meet, if at all, only in a nightmare. All day long we
are, in some degree, helping each other to one or other of
these destinations. . . . There are no ordinary people. You
have never talked to a mere mortal. Nations, cultures, arts,
civilization—these are mortal, and their life is to ours as
the life of a gnat. But it is immortals whom we joke with,
work with, marry, snub, and exploit—immortal horrors or
everlasting splendors.[34]

Ransom realizes that Tinidril is getting worn down by the Unman's unscrupulous tactics. He keeps saying to himself, "This can't go on." And the answer that comes back is "Precisely." He finally realizes that he is simply called upon to stop it. To do so would not be an imposition of a "might makes right" ethic over the disinterested search for truth because the Unman cares nothing for Truth and uses Reason only as a pragmatic tool that he drops as soon as it no longer suits him. To allow the debate to continue would in fact under those terms be to permit a kind of rhetorical rather than physical "might makes right" to triumph unopposed. Tinidril will not be allowed to be tempted beyond what she is able to bear. So Maleldil casts the Green Lady and all of Perelandra into a deep sleep, and Ransom, in a horrible battle that almost destroys him, kills the Unman, and creates a memorial to Weston. As a result both of his contributions to the debate and of this action, Perelandra is saved. Having resisted the temptation, the Green Lady moves beyond it. She now sees through the arguments of the enemy, and they are no more a danger to her. The insights Ransom was able to contribute during the debates become in retrospect a part of that new maturity. She is reunited with Tor, her husband; the prohibition of sleeping on the fixed land is repealed as having served its purpose, and she is reunited with a now healed Ransom before the eldila come to return him to Earth. Here Ransom meets Tor, the Adam figure, for the first time, in a passage that demands to be quoted in full. For there is no fuller revelation of Lewis's insight into the essence of our humanity than this.

> The eyes of the Queen looked upon him with love and recognition, but it was not of the Queen that he thought most. It was hard to think of anything but the King. And how shall I—I who have not seen him—tell you what he was like? It was hard even for Ransom to tell me of the King's face. But we dare not withhold the truth. It was that face which no man can say he does not know. You might ask how it was possible to look upon it and not to commit idolatry, not to mistake it for that of which it was the likeness. For the resemblance was, in its own fashion,

infinite, so that almost you could wonder at finding no
sorrows in his brow and no wounds in his hands and feet.
Yet there was no danger of mistaking, not one moment
of confusion, no least sally of the will towards forbidden
reverence. Where likeness was greatest, mistake was least
possible. Perhaps this is always so. A clever wax-work can
be made so like a man that for a moment it deceives us:
the great portrait which is far more deeply like him does
not. Plaster images of the Holy One may before now have
drawn to themselves the adoration they were meant to
arouse for the reality. But here, where His live image, like
Him within and without, made by His own bare hands
out of the depth of divine artistry, His masterpiece of self-
portraiture coming forth from His workshop to delight all
worlds, walked and spoke before Ransom's eyes, it could
never be taken for more than an image. Nay, the very
beauty of it lay in the certainty that it was a copy, like and
not the same, an echo, a rhyme, an exquisite reverberation
of the uncreated music prolonged in a created medium.[35]

Because Maleldil the Young had become a man in the redemption
of Ransom's people, all hnau will now be created in that image. So
while Tor is not human, he is an image of perfected humanity precisely
because he is a portrait of Christ. No conception of humanity can ever
be accurate or complete which does not see Christ as the template for
the perfection of our nature. So as Tor is, so those who are redeemed
by faith in Christ are becoming. All men and women are portraits of
Christ—not clones but unique artistic renderings—each designed to
bring out on the finite plane certain features of the infinitely majestic
and gracious original. Fallen men are still portraits, some still fairly
recognizable, but they have been corrupted into caricatures who can
make that face leer at us in a Satanic parody which insults and demeans

the model rather than bringing out its glories. Redeemed men and women are portraits being restored to their original beauty.

I said that, as Tor is, redeemed humanity will be. But not quite. God's infinite creativity is able, while always working according to the same, recognizable pattern of grace and splendor, never to do the same thing twice. Sunrise is always sunrise, the seasons always the same seasons, but always new, never a mere repetition of what has gone before. In the same way perfected Perelandran hnau is like perfected humanity but not a repetition of it. The image of Christ has sorrows in its brow and wounds in its hands and feet which it shares with us alone. Tor and Tinidril are the good we might have been now being allowed to be, but they are not exactly the good that awaits us. For the good God brings out of evil is in the long run a more impressive tribute to his grace and exemplar of his glory than it could have been otherwise. Those sorrows and those wounds as the foundation of our joy give it a depth that even the holy angels can envy and into which they long to look. And therefore, the only possible words with which we can close this section on *Perelandra* are the ones which echo so insistently through the last pages of that book:

Blessed be he!

That Hideous Strength

It might appear that anything Lewis could do after *Perelandra* would be an anticlimax. And indeed many readers have found the last volume of the trilogy, *That Hideous Strength,* a mixed success. It is the Lewis book that most shows the influence of the more eccentric and esoteric mind of Charles Williams, which was held by Tolkien to have "spoiled" it.[36] In it Lewis achieves a new psychological depth of character development that foreshadows *'Till We Have Faces,* puts a fascinating spin on the Arthurian legend, further develops his own original planetary mythology, creates a compellingly prophetic dystopia to rival *1984* and *Brave New World*, and writes a "spiritual thriller" that does indeed compare favorably with Charles Williams. Each of these elements is fascinating in its own right, but one may question whether they cohere to form an artistic unity as aesthetically satisfying as *Perelandra* or *'Till We Have Faces*. Whether or no, the book is certainly worth reading, and while it cannot recapture the profundity of *Perelandra*, it does give us useful insights into the nature of the challenges to the conception of human nature and destiny captured so poignantly there. It has often and with accuracy been called a fictional incarnation of the expository warnings in *The Abolition of Man*. That is why Francis Schaeffer said, "I strongly urge Christians to read carefully this prophetic piece of science fiction."[37]

After his return from Perelandra, Ransom becomes the "director" of a little community of people at the manor of St. Anne's. Their purpose is to monitor and oppose the designs of our own dark eldila here on Thulcandra. Those designs involve the creation of the "materialist magician" that Lewis had warned about in *Screwtape*.[38] The National Institute for Coordinated Experiments (N.I.C.E.), a new government bureaucracy, is their front. The stated purpose of the Institute is the coordination of scientific effort for the benefit of mankind. Its real purpose, unknown to all but a handful, is to prepare the planet for conquest by the dark eldila, or "macrobes." There are two means to this end. First, they are keeping alive the severed head of the criminal Alcasan, which, like the Unman of Perelandra, is the instrument through which their real masters speak to them. Second, they are trying to take over Bracton College, ostensibly as a base of operations but really because the college owns Bragdon Wood, where the body of the ancient sorcerer Merlin lies hidden in suspended animation. Believing Merlin to have been a black magician using the powers of the Bent One, they wish to revive him and enlist him in their cause. The company at St. Anne's wishes to prevent this plan from succeeding.

All this is revealed gradually through the, at first, very normal and mundane-seeming lives of Mark and Jane Studdock. Mark is a fellow of Bracton in sociology who is recruited and is slowly being corrupted by the N.I.C.E. Jane, his wife, trying desperately to be a liberated modern woman, is finishing a dissertation on Donne. But she has disturbing dreams which are prophecies of what is coming. A friend recommends that she go to St. Anne's for help in dealing with them, and she finds herself, against all her modernist training and prejudices, being drawn into that company and becoming part of its plans. Thus the stage is set for the final conflict between darkness and light.

At this point the book makes a radical shift of style and even genre. It starts out as a modern, realistic, psychological novel, and suddenly shifts into a fantastic mode that at points almost borders on the farcical. But what seems to some readers a fault of artistic unity is in its own way essential to the larger design, as even those who do not view its execution as completely successful need to understand. Lewis builds up an ordinary world of personal consciousness and institutional intrigue with meticulous and painstaking detail so that he can show the supernatural breaking into precisely that unremarkable ordinariness with something like the shock we should experience if such a thing really happened. In the meantime we get portraits of two different philosophies of life embodied not only in the speeches of their proponents but also in the organization, tone, and ambience of two communities. Finally, Merlin turns out against all hopes and fears to be on the side of light; Ransom is revealed as the Pendragon, successor to Arthur, and his company as the faithful remnant of Logres (Arthurian Britain); Mark, in revulsion at the perversions of the N.I.C.E. after all his attempts to insinuate himself into it, is converted as their efforts to pervert him backfire; Merlin goes to Belbury (the N.I.C.E. headquarters) and helps to push it to the logical conclusions of its own philosophy, with the result that all hell breaks loose there, and it self-destructs; and Mark and Jane are reunited as all heaven breaks loose at St. Anne's.

One of the central questions of *Abolition* that plays a central role in *That Hideous Strength* is that of whether and to what extent man is reducible to either his physical components or to the laws of physics or to other concepts derived from a materialist scientific model. This is the irony of the materialist magician: though one might think the Belbury Inner Circle's contact with the Macrobes would remind them of man's spiritual and therefore irreducible nature, it does not because they have become captive to the bent eldila's point of view, which is the ultimate reductionism. The Bent One cares nothing for man or for men; he himself had long ago reduced everything to power. Scientific reductionism, in a way, is just one more form of that reduction: for every action (power) there is an equal and opposite reaction. That is why Bill the Blizzard, a Bracton traditionalist who has an "unfortunate accident" as a result of his opposition to the N.I.C.E., objects in principle to the social sciences. He maintains that there is no such thing as a social science, not because we cannot learn anything useful from such study but because he opposes any attempt to subsume humanity under a scientific paradigm that carries with it the assumption that it is possible to gain an exhaustive understanding of human beings that way. "That's what happens when you study men: you find mare's nests. I happen to believe that you can't study men: you can only get to know them, which is quite a different thing."[39]

Mark's education in sociology by contrast has had the effect of teaching him to reduce humanity to statistics. Now, we must acknowledge that Lewis's critique of social science as a discipline has become somewhat dated. New methods involving more holistic approaches and qualitative analysis coming into greater prominence have blunted the edge of his satire a bit. But whether they have essentially altered the reductionist nature of the enterprise is an open question. And the mentality Lewis described in Mark is definitely still with us, along with its concomitant addiction to jargon. "His education had had the curious effect of making things that he read and wrote more real to him than things he saw. Statistics about agricultural laborers were the substance; any real ditcher, ploughman, or farmer's boy, was the shadow. Though he had never noticed it himself, he had a great reluctance, in his work, ever to use such words as 'man' or 'woman.' He preferred to write about 'vocational groups,' 'elements,' 'classes' and 'populations': for, in his own way, he believed as firmly as any mystic in the superior reality of the things that are not seen."[40] This tendency to manipulate human beings in terms of mathematical abstractions makes it easy for Mark to learn to lie for the Institute as an instrument of its propaganda. Without the Tao, abstractions are too weak to stand against the actual reality behind the Institute: the drive for power.

That drive for power is what everything ultimately reduces to if the Tao is rejected, as postmodernism rightly understands. Unfortunately, like the N.I.C.E., postmodernists too often do not lament this fact but rather embrace it. The inner circle at the Institute is willing to dabble even in demonism, which is what their alliance with the Macrobes boils down to, because it seems the path to ultimate power. But once we have made power our god, no room is left for democracy or human rights—much less humanity.

"It is the beginning of Man Immortal and Man Ubiquitous," said Straik. "Man on the throne of the universe. It is what all the prophecies really mean."

"At first, of course," said Filostrato, "the power will be confined to a number—a small number—of individual men. Those who are selected for eternal life."

"And you mean," said Mark, "it will then be extended to all men?"

"No," said Filostrato. "I mean it will then be reduced
to one man. You are not a fool, are you, my young friend?
All that talk about the power of Man over Nature—Man
in the abstract—is only for the *canaglia*. You know as well
as I do that Man's power over Nature means the power of
some men over other men with Nature as the instrument.
There is no such thing as Man—it is a word. There are
only men. No! It is not Man who will be omnipotent, it is
some one man, some immortal man. Alcasan, our Head, is
the first sketch of it. The completed product may be someone else. It may be you. It may be me."[41]

Whoever it is, it will mean disaster and dehumanization for everyone
else.

Surely one lesson of modernism is that a misplaced trust in
scientific objectivity leads to cynicism about all objective truth. In a
prescient passage which uncannily presages the more negative forms
of postmodernism, Lewis laments:

The physical sciences, good and innocent in themselves, had already, even in Ransom's own time, begun
to be warped, had been subtly manoeuvred in a certain
direction. Despair of objective truth had been increasingly insinuated into the scientists; indifference to it, and a
concentration upon mere power, had been the result. . . .
Perhaps few or none of the people at Belbury knew what
was happening; but once it happened, they would be like
straw in fire. What should they find incredible, since they
believed no longer in a rational universe? What should they
regard as too obscene, since they held that all morality was
a mere subjective by-product of the physical and economic
situations of men? The time was ripe.[42]

In the self-consciously postmodern world the "concentration on
mere power" that proceeds from despair of objective truth has been

extended to every discipline. All truth claims have been dissolved into an endless flood of jargon; all ideas are dismissed by being "situated" in the all-powerful web of period, race, class, and gender; all ideals are explained away as the futile attempts of dead white European males to hang on to power. The acid of the hermeneutic of suspicion has eaten away at the fabric of knowledge until it can no longer hold anything together. Packer accurately describes what we are left with as "spirituality without truth, individuality without restraints, pluralistic pragmatism, whimsy claiming to be wisdom, desire masquerading as morality, and benevolent tolerance of any and every view that does not tell you that you yourself are wrong."[43] Lewis's prophecy could not have been more accurate if he had been able to read an advance copy of Derrida in the 1940s!

The politics at both Bracton and Belbury reflect the brilliant analysis of individual and group psychology that Lewis gave us in his essay "*The Inner Ring.*" Mark wants desperately to validate his existence by becoming part of the inner circle, the people really "in the know," first in the college and then in the Institute. He will do anything to impress Devine, Frost, and Wither and then anything to avoid being excluded from their circle once admitted, including breaches of professional ethics and what ultimately amounts to helping them set up a totalitarian police state. As he is brought further in, in a demonic parody of the "further up and further in!" of Narnia, he has to undergo what is called "objectivity training," though it is ironically designed to make him impervious to any kind of real objectivity such as might come from being rooted in the *Tao*. This training and his reactions to it are one of the major themes of the second half of the book. Its goal is to make him precisely a man without a chest, to train him to think about all traditional values that might stand in the way of the Institute's objectives as the authors of *The Green Book* would think: "It is, again, to promote objectivity. A circle bound together by subjective feelings of mutual confidence and liking would be useless. Those, as I have said, are chemical phenomena. They could all in principle be produced by injections. You have been made to pass through a number of conflicting feelings about the Deputy Director and others in order that your future association with us may not be based on feelings at all."[44]

When Mark hesitates, "It—it seems rather a formidable decision," he is told, "that is merely a proposition about the state of your own body at the moment."[45] Once we are no longer making statements about waterfalls, but they are reduced to our own feelings only, which are further reduced to biochemical reactions, then there is no longer any possible ethical ground for objecting to whatever atrocities the Institute may feel are necessary to achieve its objectives.[46] It really seems as if his teachers are succeeding in making Mark into a convinced postmodernist fifty years in advance, sophisticatedly "situating" all statements of traditional value in history so as to rob them of any potential validity for the present. As Frost explains, "In reality the question [of right or wrong] is meaningless. It presupposes a means-and-end pattern of thought which descends from Aristotle, who in his turn was merely hypostatising elements in the experience of an iron-age agricultural community."[47] Mark then "saw clearly that the motives on which most men act, and which they dignify by the names of patriotism or duty to humanity, were mere products of the animal organism, varying according to the behaviour pattern of different communities. But he did not yet see what was to be substituted for these irrational motives. On what ground henceforward were actions to be justified or condemned?"[48]

A good question but not one his mentors will want to answer. For without the *Tao*, the only answer they can give is that whatever is, is right. "'If one insists on putting the question in those terms,' said Frost, 'I think Waddington has given the best answer. Existence is its own justification. The tendency to developmental change which we call Evolution is justified by the fact that it is a general characteristic of biological entities. The present establishment of contact between the highest biological entities and the Macrobes is justified by the fact that it is occurring, and it ought to be increased because an increase is taking place.'"[49]

The implications of this answer are not lost on Mark. "You think, then," said Mark, "that there would be no sense in asking whether the general tendency of the universe might be in the direction we should call Bad?" Frost has learned well the lessons of Gaius and Titius: "There could be no sense at all," said Frost. "The judgment you are trying to make turns out on inspection to be simply an expression of emotion."[50] And the reader hopefully realizes that Frost has just sawed off the very limb he is sitting on. If good and bad are only subjective feelings, not real objective realities, then you cannot say it is better or more accurate to say that the man was making a statement about his own feelings rather than about the waterfall. Nor can you say even that mere expressions of emotion "ought" to be discounted. You can only say that you prefer to say it that way and that you are the head of the tenure committee, so there. Might makes right, and that is the end of the story. So if we happen to have the might, or can sneak it away from naïve and unsuspecting secular scholars who have actually swallowed our insincere rhetoric about tolerance, we might as well use it. More power to us.

Frost, like all Nietscheans, has built his intellectual house of cards so well that it cannot help falling apart. And so it is that at this point Mark's training begins to backfire. His memories of life with Jane, of a time before he began to sell his soul for this mess of epistemological pottage and moral twistedness, begin to come back to him. He realizes that Frost simply cannot be right.

And day by day, as the process went on, that idea of the Straight or the Normal which had occurred to him during his first visit to this room, grew stronger and more solid in his mind till it had become a kind of mountain. He had never before known what an Idea meant: he had always thought till now that they were things inside one's own head. But now, when his head was continually attacked and often completely filled with the clinging corruption of the training, this Idea towered up above him—something which obviously existed quite independently of himself and had hard rock surfaces which would not give, surfaces he could cling to.[51]

This movement in the story comes to its climax when as the "final exam" of his training Mark is asked to desecrate a crucifix to prove that he has finally been set free from any pull toward the "tyranny" of traditional value (the *Tao*). At this moment his doubts about the whole process coalesce into a kind of certainty. In a speech laden with dramatic irony, conveying insight far beyond anything he could yet know that he knows, he refuses. "I'm damned if I do any such thing."[52] And he would have been. But he does not do it, and so the turning point in what will eventually become his conversion has been reached. Rejecting the void, he turns back to the *Tao* and thereby begins to recapture his own humanity.

In the N.I.C.E., Lewis gave us an interesting picture of what modernism would look like if its seeds were ever allowed to sprout and grow unchecked. Denniston asks whether there was anything they did that had not been blithely taught for years by university professors like Gaius and Titius. "Oh, of course, they never thought any one would *act* on their theories! No one was more astonished than they when what they'd been talking of for years suddenly took on reality. But it was their own child coming back to them: grown up and unrecognizable, but their own."[53]

What is also interesting is the way this picture of modernism gone to seed becomes eerily prophetic of some forms of what is ironi- cally called postmodernism. It would seem that many postmodernists are not as liberated from modernism or beyond it as they would like to think. While postmodernism no longer "privileges" science and the scientific method as giving us a unique access to objectivity and truth (which we must recognize as a genuine advance), it is too often united with late modernism in its common rejection of the objective existence of the *Tao* and therefore (unlike modernism, which was in this sense less consistent) of the possibility of any kind of objective knowledge of truth or value on *any* basis. In this respect we could accurately define *postmodernism* as "modernism gone to seed."[54] The modernist is in many ways a posthumanist, and modernism is, in its reductionist tendencies, subhuman. Therefore, insofar as it involves an even more radical rejection of the *Tao*, we may also say that to be postmodern (i.e., really ultramodern or hypermodern) is to be, in a sense prophesied by *The Abolition of Man*, posthuman.

Meanwhile, the good eldila, working through Merlin, cause the N.I.C.E. to self-destruct in a great cataclysm. Mark escapes and is reunited with Jane at St. Anne's, which seems to be particularly under the influence of the Oyarsa of Perelandra (Venus). In an obedience which involves a reaffirmation of masculinity and femininity, the richness of humanity is being restored after the barrenness of Belbury. "She comes more near the Earth than she was wont to—to make Earth sane. Perelandra is all about us, and man is no longer isolated. We are now as we ought to be—between the angels who are our elder brothers and the beasts who are our jesters, servants and playfellows."[55] The attempt to abolish man has failed for now. But the ideologies which drove it still have power and must continue to be opposed. Fortunately, in that light, the ending of the book highlights one more truth about what it means to be human: we are not on our own.

Blessed be he.

Interlude

EARTH

Villanelle No. 14

The origin and ground of all who grieve
  Is ground we walk on, kicking as we go
The bones of Adam and the flesh of Eve.
Dust to dust, the day they took their leave
  They sowed the bitter seed of death and woe
Deep in the fertile ground of all who grieve.
We reap the thorns and thistles, we receive
  The harvest, and within us still we grow
The bones of Adam and the flesh of Eve.
With all our efforts, all we can achieve
  Is to extend the seedbeds, row on row,
Planted in the ground of all who grieve.
The winds take up the dust, the winds that weave
  Their way around the world, and there they blow
The bones of Adam and the flesh of Eve.
We look away; we'd rather not believe.
  Still, none who walks the earth can help but know
  The origin and ground of all who grieve:
The bones of Adam and the flesh of Eve.

—D.T.W.

Chapter Five

THE ABOLITION OF TALKING BEASTS

Perspectives on the Human in The Chronicles of Narnia

"Beasts did leap and birds did sing,
Trees did grow and plants did spring."
—SHAKESPEARE, "THE PASSIONATE PILGRIM"

WHILE HIS ADULT FICTION, his literary scholarship, his poetry, and his rational Christian apologetics all have lasting value, there is a growing consensus that C. S. Lewis's most enduring legacy will be his children's stories, The Chronicles of Narnia. They have already won a spot alongside those rare books like *The Wind in the Willows* that work wonderfully well as children's fiction but cannot be left behind when one becomes an adult—indeed, probably cannot be fully appreciated until then. I personally did not read them for the first time until I was a college student already depending on *Mere Christianity, Miracles,* and The Space Trilogy as part of my necessary

food. "Children's stories?" I sniffed skeptically in my freshman pseu-
domaturity. Well, no doubt if Lewis wrote them, they will be worth
a cursory glance, I conceded. And then I lost an entire night's sleep
hungrily devouring them one after another. It was a good trade.

I would have to say that the greatest work of mythopoeic fiction
overall is without question Tolkien's Lord of the Rings. Its depth and
consistency satisfy mind and heart like nothing else. But the Narnia
books are original and creative in their own way: "There may have
been a wicked witch in fairy tale (beautiful too, as in "Snow White"),
but there has never been a divine lion, nor a journey by ship to the
uttermost east, nor the making and the destruction of a world; and
nothing in fairy tale could prepare us for a Marsh-wiggle."[1]

They have an ability to get under one's skin that is simply
unmatched. (This ability is enhanced, by the way, when they are read
in their original publication order, not the chronological ordering
that has replaced it in recent editions due to a tragic misapplication of
one of Lewis's offhand comments.[2]) I have never read them without
at some point being reduced to helpless tears, usually by a different
and unexpected passage that hits me from out of nowhere with an
intense blast of what Lewis called Joy.[3]

Unlike the Field of Arbol of the Space Trilogy, which is a version of the actual solar system we inhabit, Narnia is part of a parallel
universe with its own separate space and time. It is the land of talking
beasts, hnau that have the forms (and "personalities") of familiar terran animals augmented or magnified. So naturally the Lord of that
world, the form the Creator takes when he reveals himself to it, is
the king of beasts, Aslan the wondrous golden lion, son of the great
Emperor-Beyond-the-Sea.

The Chronicles of Narnia are full of passages that wonderfully incarnate for the imagination many of the basic ideas we have
expounded for the reason in our study of works like *The Everlasting
Man* and *The Abolition of Man,* and by doing so make them clearer to

the reason as well. Could anything, for example, put all we have said about reductionism into a more compact and potent nutshell than this little exchange: "In our world," said Eustace, "a star is a huge ball of flaming gas." Ramandu replies, "Even in your world, my son, that is not what a star is but only what it is made of."[4] Or think of Lucy's experience as an encapsulization of the philosophy of stories: "'This is a very queer book. How can I have forgotten? It was about a cup and a sword and a tree and a green hill, I know that much. But I can't remember and what *shall* I do?' And she never could remember; and ever since that day what Lucy means by a good story is a story which reminds her of the forgotten story in the Magician's Book."[5]

But perhaps the most interesting insights about who we are as human beings come from the characters themselves and the ways they interact. Those interactions are themselves part of the message. Manlove notes how "great value is placed on meeting and society: the child protagonists are almost always shown in pairs or groups. In *The Lion* and *The Voyage* the quests link up the separated parts of a country, or the isolated egos on islands. Those who live alone . . . are either evil or at risk of becoming so—the witch, King Miraz, the Tisroc of Calormen, Prince Rilian in *The Silver Chair*."[6] As in Perelandra, the solidarity of the race is pictured in practical terms. Also significant are the interactions between individuals of different races.

Aslan's talking beasts contrast both with the dumb beasts of Narnia and with the human children (sons of Adam and daughters of Eve) from England who are sent to Narnia by magic, not just to have various adventures but to play a leading role in Narnian history—to be, in fact, kings and queens of Narnia. Apparently the principle from Perelandra that the incarnation of the Son of God as man in our world caused a cosmic corner to be turned, affecting all worlds from then on applies to parallel universes as well as other planets. For Narnia functions properly only when human beings rule, not just beasts in general, but—in a different way, of course—talking beasts as well. It was a prophecy trusted in by the faithful during the long winter imposed by the White Witch (when it was always winter but never Christmas): "When Adam's flesh and Adam's bone / Sits at Cair Paravel in throne, / The evil time will be over and done."[7]

So basic is this principle that even Jadis, the Witch, must pretend to be human in order to perpetuate her tyranny. "Isn't the Witch herself human?" the children ask. "She'd like us to believe it," said Mr. Beaver, "and it's on that that she bases her claim to be Queen. But she's no Daughter of Eve."[8] She is descended from giant and Jinn, and her claim is fraudulent. All right order is perverted when Adam's descendants do not rule by Aslan's gift—even in this other world. "There was something in his face and air which no one could mistake. That look is in the face of all true Kings of Narnia, who rule by the will of Aslan and sit at Cair Paravel on the throne of Peter the High King."[9] Shades of Shakespeare's Kent: "There is that in thy countenance which I would fain call master."

Because they are fallen, the rule of human beings does not guarantee right order, as the career of Miraz the Usurper proves; to be human is not necessarily to rule by Aslan's will. But though not a sufficient condition, it is a necessary one, emphasized in more than one book. "'Don't you go talking about things you don't under-stand, Nikabrik,' said Trufflehunter. 'You Dwarfs are as forgetful and changeable as the Humans themselves. I'm a beast, I am, and a Badger what's more. We don't change. We hold on. I say great good will come of it. This is the true King of Narnia we've got here: a true King, coming back to true Narnia. And we beasts remember, even if Dwarfs forget, that Narnia was never right except when a Son of Adam was King.'"[10]

Thus, even though Narnia is not a land untouched by evil, it sometimes rises in a limited way to a recapturing of the Edenic rela-tionship between man and beast pictured and lamented in Perelandra.

Frank and Helen, Peter, Edmund, Susan, and Lucy are a picture of man's benevolent rule over creation, but they are not a simple picture. Human beings in general are related to talking beasts in general as equals, as befits the relationship of hnau to hnau. "'Why do you keep talking to my horse instead of to me?' asked the girl. 'Excuse me, Tarkheena,' said Bree (with just the slightest backward tilt of his ears), 'but that's Calormene talk. We're free Narnians, Hwin and I, and I suppose, if you're running away to Narnia, you want to be one too. In that case Hwin isn't *your* horse any longer. One might just as well say you're *her* human.'"[11]

In modern terms all hnau have equal value as created persons and hence equal standing and equal rights before the law. But even though the Narnian talking beasts are created equal with human beings as hnau and are endowed by their Creator, as it were, with certain inalienable rights, still it is Sons of Adam and Daughters of Eve who belong on the throne, and Narnia only functions properly when the chosen ones are there.

How can humans and talking beasts be equal, and yet humans are supposed to rule? That is the critical question for moderns reading the Narnia books. And the answer is a key to many things. There is perhaps a hint here that man's position of dominion over Narnia (and, by implication, Earth) is not necessarily based on his superiority. That is, perhaps man was given the superior gifts of language and reason that make his dominion over the animals possible because of his position, not given the position because he had superior gifts. This is not a trivial distinction. The whole traditional Christian conception of leadership functions in a healthy way only when we grasp it. Trying to apply it without grasping this truth can turn male headship in the home, for example, into the tyranny that feminism so rightly objects to.

Secular thinking assumes that *leadership* (one aspect of the richer biblical idea of *headship*) is a form of superiority so that subordination

necessarily entails inferiority. Hence Jesus observes that the kings of
the Gentiles "lord it over them" and feel justified in doing so. But
for his disciples he stipulates that it should not be so, but rather the
greatest should be among them as a servant (Luke 22:25–27). In the
upper room he makes himself an example of this principle, washing
the disciples' feet and then asking them, "Do you understand what
I have done?" (John 13:12). They rightly call him master and lord,
but they will not understand what that means until they learn to
follow his example of servant leadership.

This watershed of divergent assumptions causes much misunderstanding between the church and the surrounding society (and increasingly much misunderstanding even within the church), especially in the
modern West. Secular people, operating according to what we might call
the "Gentile paradigm" of Luke 22, cannot help but perceive the New
Testament teaching on male headship as demeaning to women, implying for them a position of inferiority based on an actual assumption of
inferiority. (Christian denials that this is what the Bible means, or what
they mean, often simply fail to register. There is no sticking place for
such an idea in the secular mind.) This impression is compounded by
the fact that the Gentile paradigm has subtly infiltrated the church as
well, with the result that some of the defenders of the traditional view,
well-meaning but misguided, try to defend it based on males' alleged
better suitedness for leadership—as if that came first. Even Lewis is
capable of falling into this trap, in one of the least convincing sections
of *Mere Christianity*.[12] All this being true, it is not surprising that the
actual practice of headship in both home and church too often tragically
confirms the erroneous conclusions of the secular observer. But one who
truly understands the biblical ethos realizes that it need not be so, indeed
must not be so if we are to be faithful to the teaching and example of
our Lord.

We are all free Narnians, in other words, and those to whom the
burden of leadership is given must not forget it. They are called to

be servants and must not assume an aura of superiority. "For this is what it means to be a king," says Lune: "To be first in every desperate attack and last in every desperate retreat, and when there's hunger in the land (as must be now and then in bad years) to wear finer clothes and laugh louder over a scantier meal than any man in your land."[13] Part of King Frank's qualifications for the job is his humility: "I ain't no sort of chap for a job like that."[14] His lack of "eddycation" is no disbarment. What Aslan really wants to know is, "Can you rule these creatures kindly and fairly, remembering that they are not slaves like the dumb beasts of the world you were born in, but Talking Beasts and free subjects?"[15] The deportment of the good Narnian kings with their subjects is a picture that may help to rebaptize our imaginations in this area.

There is no romanticism here, though, about the relations between man and animal. The dumb beasts are properly called "slaves." We must again realize that, given Lewis's use of this term in Perelandra, we must bracket many of the connotations the word has for us if we are to understand him. But the instinct that gives us that reaction is a sound one. It is wrong to make slaves of human beings precisely because they *are* human beings. We must not use hnau so even if we do not mistreat them. But that does not mean that we can safely transfer our strong negative feelings about human slavery into a realm where they are not applicable or appropriate.

To make slaves of human beings—or talking beasts—*is* to mistreat them because it is to deny their God-given nature and force them to live a lie. The great evil this does to them is not so much the curtailment of their freedom in itself as the fact that the lie lived tends to take on reality in their lives, as Bree discovers. "One of the worst results of being a slave and being forced to do things is that when there is no one to force you any more you find you have almost lost the power of forcing yourself."[16] That is because the power of self-determination is one of the characteristics that is distinctive of hnau as opposed to other animals. (It is sometimes called *free will*, a designation that can seem more controversial than it really is. All Christians agree that it is a defining characteristic of created human nature; they disagree only about how far it was forfeited in the Fall.) But we properly have dominion over the beasts, who find a part of the fulfillment of their God-given natures in serving us. This distinction is basic and is understood by talking beasts as well as humans, if not by dwarfs like Nikabrik.

"'He has *hunted* beasts for sport. Haven't you, now?' he added, rounding suddenly on Caspian.

"'Well, to tell you the truth, I have,' said Caspian. 'But they weren't Talking Beasts.'

"'It's all the same thing,' said Nikabrik.

"'No, no, no,' said Trufflehunter. 'You know it isn't.'"[17]

Indeed, the talking beasts have a relation to the dumb ones that is similar to ours: "Creatures, I give you yourselves," said the strong, happy voice of Aslan. "I give to you forever this land of Narnia. I give you the woods, the fruits, the rivers. I give you the stars and I give you myself. The Dumb Beasts whom I have not chosen are yours also. Treat them gently and cherish them but do not go back to their ways lest you cease to be Talking Beasts. For out of them you were taken and into them you can return. Do not so."[18]

The talking beasts receive this relationship by the manner of their creation, in a passage that cries out to be quoted in full:

And now, for the first time, the Lion was quite silent. He was going to and fro among the animals. And every now and then he would go up to two of them (always two at a time) and touch their noses with his. He would touch two beavers among all the beavers, two leopards among all the leopards, one stag and one deer among all the deer, and leave the rest. Some sorts of animal he passed over altogether. But the pairs which he had touched instantly

left their own kinds and followed him. At last he stood
still and all the creatures whom he had touched came
and stood in a wide circle around him. The others whom
he had not touched began to wander away. Their noises
faded gradually into the distance. The chosen beasts who
remained were now utterly silent, all with their eyes fixed
intently upon the Lion. The cat-like ones gave an occa-
sional twitch of the tail but otherwise all were still. For the
first time that day there was complete silence, except for
the noise of running water. Digory's heart beat wildly; he
knew something very solemn was going to be done. He
had not forgotten about his Mother; but he knew jolly well
that, even for her, he couldn't interrupt a thing like this.

The Lion, whose eyes never blinked, stared at the animals as hard as if he was going to burn them up with his
mere stare. And gradually a change came over them. The
smaller ones—the rabbits, moles, and such-like—grew a
good deal larger. The very big ones—you noticed it most
with the elephants—grew a little smaller. Many animals
sat up on their hind legs. Most put their heads on one side
as if they were trying very hard to understand. The Lion
opened his mouth, but no sound came from it; he was
breathing out, a long, warm breath; it seemed to sway all
the beasts as the wind sways a line of trees. Far overhead
from beyond the veil of blue sky which hid them the stars
sang again; a pure, cold, difficult music. Then there came
a swift flash like fire (but it burnt nobody) either from the
sky or from the Lion itself, and every drop of blood tingled
in the children's bodies, and the deepest, wildest voice they
had ever heard was saying:

"Narnia, Narnia, Narnia, awake. Love. Think. Speak.
Be walking trees. Be talking beasts. Be divine waters."[19]

The Talking Beasts are taken from the ranks of the dumb ones, much as Adam and Eve were taken from the dust of the earth. This is an important point. It reminds us that there is a real level of solidarity we share with the dumb beasts, exclusive concentration on which makes reductionism possible. In scientific terms, we might (with Lewis and Chesterton) conceive of evolution as contributing to the form of our bodies; we cannot believe that it accounts for our minds. In biblical terms, we, like the beasts, were formed from the dust of the ground. It also pictures the fact that what differentiates us from the dumb beasts is not to be found in physiology. The changes in size they undergo are not changes in *form* (in the Aristotelian sense), and are there, I think, for the purpose primarily of facilitating their intelligent and articulate interactions with humans, who occupy the middle point in size between mole and elephant.

The difference is the breath of Aslan. "The Lord God . . . breathed into his nostrils the breath of life, and the man became a living being" (Gen. 2:7). It is not having one more convolution in our brains nor possessing opposable thumbs that makes us human; it is a *donum superaditum*, an additional gift, which is ultimately spiritual. Its result is that we, like the Spirit whose breath both conveys and is the gift, can love, think, and speak. The higher does not stand without the lower: the animals exchange affection (*storge*), perform rudimentary problem solving, and use noises and other signals for communication by instinct. But talking beasts and humans do it with understanding (for when the flash came, the heads tilted to one side were rewarded), and hence may rise to *philadelphia* or even *agape*, to the lives examined by reason that constitute the wisdom of philosophy, and to the form of linguistic self-awareness that is grammar, logic, rhetoric, and even poetry. And so the talking beasts, by the gift of Aslan, are enabled to respond: "Hail, Aslan. We hear and obey. We are awake. We love. We think. We speak. We know."[20]

The talking beasts emerge from the ranks of the dumb by the gift and grace of Aslan, but they are warned that to those ranks they may return, and they are commanded not to do so. Here we have the Narnian way of dealing with the concern Lewis raised in his expository title, *The Abolition of Man*. Lucy asks, "Wouldn't it be dreadful if some day in our own world, at home, men started going wild inside, like the animals here, and still looked like men, so that you'd never know which were which?"[21] To fall into evil—to separate oneself from the only Source of our ability to love, think, and speak, and try to live outside his authority—is to compromise one's humanity. It is not to destroy it, not finally at least until that irrevocable destruction, which is the hell pictured in Weston's decayed mind; but it is most definitely to corrupt it and to put it at risk. Secular reductionist philosophies such as those critiqued in *Abolition* serve to hasten and encourage this loss, to insulate us from the arrestings of it built into the world by common grace, and to push it toward the irrevocable. So in Narnia, dehumanization becomes an image of the results of sin, while redemption is viewed as the restoration of full humanity. That is why the beaver warns, "But in general, take my advice, when you meet anything that's going to be human and isn't yet, or used to be human once and isn't now, or ought to be human and isn't, you keep your eyes on it and feel for your hatchet."[22] And this is pictured in both men and talking beasts.

Ginger the cat from *The Last Battle* is perhaps the most frightening example of a talking beast who loses talking beasthood as the inevitable outcome of his persistence in his rebellion against Aslan. But the most memorable picture of fall and redemption in these terms is surely Eustace, who undergoes a rather humbling transformation: "He had turned into a dragon while he was asleep. Sleeping on a dragon's hoard with greedy, dragonish thoughts in his heart, he had become a dragon himself."[23]

The basis for Eustace's transformation is found in Lewis's poem "Eden's Courtesy." Each of the animals, even terran dumb beasts, eloquently expresses a certain potential personality trait found in human beings. Certain ones are so obvious that they have become traditional, a kind of symbolic or iconographic shorthand. "For till I tame sly fox and timorous hare / And lording lion in myself, no peace / can be." It is our business not to eradicate these characteristics but to tame them, to subordinate them to reason by grace. To the extent that we fail to do so, we slip back toward the merely bestial. This is so "because the brutes within, I do not doubt, / Are archetypal of the brutes without."[24] Therefore, to the extent that we take reductionist philosophies seriously and live as if only the material exists, we dehumanize ourselves. So Carlyle was perhaps using more than just an arbitrary metaphor when he called hedonism a pig's philosophy.[25] Spenser understood this well when he had Guyon lament, "See the mind of beastly man / That hath so soone forgot the excellence / Of his creation." The Palmer (Right Reason) replies, "Let Grill be Grill and have his hoggish mind."[26]

What is in our world an archetype in Narnia can become a physical reality. So Eustace—selfish, greedy, arrogant, and cruel—becomes the actual embodiment of these qualities: he becomes a dragon. But unlike Grill, Eustace experiences his beasthood not as an act of final judgment but as an opportunity for self-understanding leading to the acceptance of mercy. He realizes that he does not like himself as a dragon, which is to say he reckons with the reality of what he was already becoming before the change, and responds in repentance. But the leopard cannot change his spots nor Eustace his scales. His own efforts to molt get him nowhere. Only by yielding himself unreservedly to Aslan can he be stripped of his dragon shape and restored to human form. And thus he becomes a moving picture not only of the necessity of grace but of the nature of redemption as restoration to full humanity.

Not everyone is so fortunate. Rabadash, who insists on making an ass of himself, becomes a donkey. And though his human form is restored, on condition that he never go more than ten miles from the temple of Tash, we surmise that this restoration is only temporary. He never humbles himself, so even though he lives out his life as a man, he is remembered even by Calormene history as Rabadash the Ridiculous, a particularly insulting way for a Calormen to refer to a Tisroc (may he live forever). So he is an ass to the end. But Aslan gives him all the mercy he will receive, as has been his wont ever since the days of Uncle Andrew: "Oh Adam's sons, how cleverly you defend yourselves against all that might do you good! But I will give him the only gift he is still able to receive."[27]

So even Rabadash's mulish refusal of redemption becomes an occasion to remind us that redemption is possible for anyone and must therefore be offered even to Rabadash. Reminded of the Calormene's treachery, "'It is very true,' said Edmund. 'But even a traitor may mend. I have known one that did.' And he looked very thoughtful."[28] For one who remembers his dalliance with the white witch and his treatment of Lucy in their first adventure, Edmund's words are among the most poignant to be found in this book or any other.

That open-endedness to our future is also, by God's grace, a part of the human condition both because we are not reducible to mere physics and even more because God has not forgotten us. "'Why, I might be anyone!' [Shasta] thought. 'I might be the son of a Tarkaan myself—or the son of the Tisroc (may he live forever)—or of a god!'"[29] And so he might. And so may we all be if we respond like Eustace to Aslan's offer to strip us of our pride and pretension. To be human is to live with the offer of that sonship or daughterhood as the destiny for which we were created and to which we can by grace be restored. And to be fully human is to be one who has accepted it.

But that awaits the future. For now the human condition involves a pilgrimage through the Shadow-Lands on a quest for Aslan's country, whether we realize that this is what we are looking for or not. It is not the human characters who give us the most profound expressions of this theme. But we have already seen that for Lewis animals can serve as natural symbols of particular human characteristics so that we not only usefully but properly describe human beings with phrases like "wise as an owl," "sly as a fox," "proud as a peacock." Thus Reepicheep, the head of the talking mice, represents the courage and devotion to honor that are really potential human virtues. In like manner Puddleglum the Marsh-wiggle is a portrait of a dour but dear faithfulness so loyal that it does not require an optimistic outlook to sustain itself. These are human virtues, but portraying them in nonhuman characters allows Lewis to present them in a distilled or concentrated form that is rarely found in human beings and probably could not be portrayed there so believably. (Compare Reepicheep, for example, with the human character who may be most like him, David Eddings' Sir Mandorallen—a most entertaining fellow, but less believable than the talking mouse.)

It falls to these characters to give the most poignant expressions of this theme of life as pilgrimage or quest. It is the final use to which Reepicheep puts his indomitable courage. Aslan is the son of the great Emperor-Beyond-the-Sea; it is always across the sea from the east that he comes to Narnia. That is ultimately why the mouse ships on the *Dawn Treader,* for its goal is to explore farther to the East than any ship in Narnian history. "While I can, I sail east in the *Dawn Treader.* When she fails me, I paddle east in my coracle. When she sinks, I shall swim east with my four paws. And when I can swim no longer, if I have not reached Aslan's country, or shot over the edge of the world in some vast cataract, I shall sink with my nose to the sunrise and Peepiceek will be head of the talking mice in

Narnia."[30] Knowing where the pearl of great price is found, Reep will sell all he has, and is, to buy that field.

Puddleglum's attitude is more down-to-earth. His quest is not for Aslan's country directly but for Narnia itself, for Overworld, which serves as an image of Aslan's country and the possibility of finding it. He has been trapped with the children in the caverns of Underworld and subjected to the reductionist propaganda of the Green Witch until he cannot even directly remember what the world of the sun is like. The sun, she tells him, is just a lamp, Aslan just a cat that he with his imagination has turned into something greater. But Puddleglum, like Lewis, sees reason to believe that imagination can be a key to reality. And besides, he will be faithful to the quest whether or not it is.

"Suppose we *have* only dreamed, or made up, all those things—trees and grass and sun and moon and stars and Aslan himself. Suppose we have. Then all I can say is that, in that case, the made-up things seem a good deal more important than the real ones. Suppose this black pit of a kingdom of yours *is* the only world. Well, it strikes me as a pretty poor one. And that's a funny thing, when you come to think of it. We're just babies making up a game, if you're right. But four babies playing a game can make a play-world which licks your real world hollow. That's why I'm going to stand by the play-world. I'm on Aslan's side even if there isn't any Aslan to lead it. I'm going to live as like a Narnian as I can even if there isn't any Narnia. So, thanking you kindly for our supper, if these two gentlemen and the young lady are ready, we're leaving your court at once and setting out in the dark to spend our lives looking for Overland. Not that our lives will be very long, I should think; but that's small loss if the world's as dull a place as you say."[31]

To be human in this age of the world is to have set out in the dark to spend one's life looking for Overland, spurred on by the "signposts" of joy that our Lord has scattered along the way.[32] To be satisfied with less, to accept wealth or fame or power as the fulfillment of one's nature, either under the influence of reductionist philosophy or just out of shallowness or discouragement, is to settle for a life that is less than fully human. It is also to turn aside from the quest that leads us to the place where our human nature is fulfilled.

Lewis's characters who do not give up the quest are destined to come to precisely that place. In *The Last Battle* Narnia falls for the deception of its Antichrist, faces its Armageddon, and is destroyed. But in that destruction the faithful find the true purpose for which Narnia was created: to make them hungry for Aslan's country and bring them there.

"It was the Unicorn who summed up what everyone was feeling. He stamped his right forehoof on the ground and neighed, and then cried:

"'I have come home at last! This is my real country! I belong here. This is the land I have been looking for all my life, though I never knew it till now. The reason why we loved the old Narnia is that it sometimes looked a little like this. Bree-hee-hee! Come further up, come further in!'"[33]

All the old characters (but one) are brought together and reunited. But most glorious of all, they are with Aslan himself, never to be separated again. The human children, for once, do not have to be sent back to England—not now or ever again.

"There *was* a real railway accident," said Aslan softly. "Your father and mother and all of you are—as you used to call it in the Shadow-lands—dead. The term is over: the holidays have begun. The dream is ended: this is the morning."

And as He spoke He no longer looked to them like a lion; but the things that began to happen after that were so great and beautiful that I cannot write them. And for us this is the end of all the stories, and we can most truly say that they all lived happily ever after. But for them it was only the beginning of the real story. All their life in this world and all their adventures in Narnia had only been the cover and the title page: now at last they were beginning Chapter One of the Great Story which no one on earth has read: which goes on forever: in which every chapter is better than the one before.[34]

One feels disinclined to dilute the eucatastrophe and the joy of such a passage by commenting on it. But we may let Tirian do so, for his words uttered in desperation were prophetic of its true meaning: "'This is my password,' said the King as he drew his sword. *The light is dawning, the lie broken.*"[35] And we may let Aslan himself do so, for in contrasting Narnia with England, he gives us the purpose for the creation not only of Narnia but also of our own world and any that may exist, and gives us at the same time our own reason for existing: "This was the very reason why you were brought to Narnia, that by knowing me here for a little, you may know me better there."[36]

Aslan also gives us the best summary we will ever find of the human condition as we now experience it: created in God's image but fallen, transcending the nature of our animal fellow creatures but capable of reducing ourselves back to it, redeemable from that supreme folly and therefore on a journey that can take us even to Aslan's country itself. "Do you mark this well?" asks Aslan.

"'I do indeed, Sir,' said Caspian. 'I was wishing that I came of a more honorable lineage.'

"'You come of the Lord Adam and the Lady Eve,' said Aslan. 'And that is both honor enough to erect the head of the poorest beggar, and shame enough to bow the shoulders of the greatest emperor on earth. Be content.'"[37]

And if we believe, then content we shall be indeed and at last.

Interlude

COMMENTARY,
GENESIS 2:19, NO. 1

Then Man, the wielder of words, awoke,
Saw the sunlight slanting down,
Saw the ground-fog swelling upward,
Heard the light laughter of leaves,
Climbed the mountains, mist-enshrouded,
Felt the wind, wet with rain,
Saw the stabbing stars in darkness,
Watched the antics of wild creatures,
Heard within his head the sounds,
Pulled them forth, in patterns ordered,
Uttered into air around him
Liquid names: in lilting language
Spoke the mighty spell of speech.

—D.T.W.

Chapter Six

THE EVERLASTING HOBBIT

Perspectives on the Human
in Tolkien's Mythos

"What seest thou else
In the dark backward and abysm of time?"
—PROSPERO, IN SHAKESPEARE'S *THE TEMPEST*

IF YOU ARE NOT YET sufficiently awed by the profound depths of which the human mind is capable through the mystery of human creativity, ponder the fact that you have just successfully read this sentence. It has a complex structure, with an independent clause and three subordinate clauses, plus four prepositional phrases. It contains thirty different words used thirty-five times. (We won't even try to think about the phonemes and morphemes!) Five of the thirty words get multiple uses: the personal pronoun *you*, the preposition *of*, forms of the verb *to be*, and the adjective *human* appear twice each, the article *the* four times; twenty-five words are used once each. The odds that you have ever seen them before combined in precisely that order are, for all practical purposes, zero. I could spend a whole chapter just analyzing that one sentence without taxing my own patience (yours is another matter). Yet I created the sentence effortlessly, and most of you probably understood it with little or no conscious effort. Both of those facts are just plain stupefying. And usually we do not even waste the adjective *creative* on expository prose of the kind I am writing now! But without this almost indescribable human capacity for creativity, language could not work. Without consciously doing any of the formal analysis (until after the fact), I spontaneously created a structure that allowed you to recreate with some accuracy in your mind the fairly complex and sophisticated meaning I was attending to in mine.

We have talked a lot in this study about man's creation in the image of God as the source of the difference between us and the rest of the animal creation. But we have hitherto been slightly vague about what the *imago Dei* is. Is it our amphibious nature combining matter and spirit, our rationality, our moral (or immoral) nature, our capacity for relationship with God; or is it simply the position we occupy as his regents, representing him as stewards and governors of creation? None of these attributes is irrelevant to the *imago*, but neither is any of them its essence. Theologians can spend interminable pages debating the details to no purpose because they have never bothered to read Genesis for its narrative flow in context.[1] When we do, the answer is plain.

The first statement that God intends to create man in his own image occurs early, in Genesis 1:26. We are in the first chapter of the first book of the Bible. So let us start from scratch. So far we have only seen two attributes of God in action; they are all that has been revealed to this point, hence all we know of him. First, he is creative; second, he is articulate. And these two facts are related: he uses language as the means of his creativity, first declaring things into existence and then giving them both form (separating light and darkness, water and land, etc.) and value (it was very good). So if we are then told that man is going to be "like" God, one would think that this likeness must refer to the only attributes that have so far been introduced into the narrative. Man, too, will be creative and articulate. And this reasonable assumption is confirmed by the story. Adam is the first creature to be *personally* addressed by God's speech; after a long string of third-person "let there be's" he is called "thou." And he immediately starts talking back. His first official act is to *create* the first human *language*: God brings the animals before him, and whatever Adam calls each one is its name. God accepts these names Adam has created and will graciously use them himself. So man, like God, is creative because he is articulate. The core of the *imago Dei* is language.

This view of the *imago* is also confirmed by what we know of language itself. It is a uniquely human creation, the one that makes all the others possible. Scientists debate whether chimps can be taught to use true language, either using Ameslan (as with Washoe) or computers (at the Yerkes Primate Center at Emory University in Atlanta). But the forms of communication these apes are observed to use in the wild do not have the open-endedness, the deep structure, or the creativity required of a true human language. If they can speak, it is only after man has been messing around with their minds. We are still the only creature who creates language spontaneously. The uniqueness of language as a human characteristic is therefore not ultimately threatened by these experiments.

Language allows us to contemplate things not immediately present in the physical environment and then to manipulate them in our heads. It is therefore the foundation of our capacity for abstract thinking and reason. Language allows us to render an account to God of our stewardship of his creation. It is therefore the foundation of the fact that, in a manner not true of the other animals, we are *accountable* for our actions, i.e., have a moral nature. That accountability allows us to function as his regents, the stewards of creation.

We see then that all the major facets of our uniqueness that have traditionally been related to the image of God find their unity in language; it is the characteristic we share with him that makes all the others possible. Like him we are creative and articulate, articulately creative and creatively articulate. We are language users because we are language makers, made in the image of the Word.[2]

It is therefore no accident that the greatest storyteller of the twentieth century, who propounded as well as practiced the theory of secondary creation, began the creation of the most believable, consistent, and compelling imaginary world ever known with the ultimate act of human creativity: the endeavor to create a language.[3] An actual language can be defined as a living and growing system which is the sum total of the creative input of each of its speakers, tempered by the creative input of all the others, to produce a shared set of dynamic conventions they can use for real communication. So Tolkien discovered that in order for Elvish to have a convincing sense of reality *as a language,* it required a people to speak it, a world for them to live in, a history and a mythology for them to remember, and other languages (spoken by neighboring peoples, who would have all the same requirements) to be related to. And that is both how we got Middle Earth and one reason it is so convincing. "Golly, what a book!" said Warren Lewis. "The inexhaustible fertility of the man's imagination amazes me."[4] Thus Tolkien's fiction exemplifies one of the central themes of our portrait of human nature simply by existing. And then there is also what it says. "J. R. R. Tolkien in his Ring trilogy sums up more powerfully than any realist could do the darkness of total war and the essential opposition of evil and good."[5]

Tolkien's fiction is not, like Lewis's, overtly Christian and even evangelistic. One of the expressed purposes for The Chronicles of Narnia is that by coming to know Aslan, there we should learn to know Christ in our own world as well.[6] Narnia is full of symbolism that borders on allegory; Middle Earth is full of plain history that is not without symbolic import.[7] There is nothing like the Stone Table east of the Sundering Sea. Nevertheless, Tolkien's book is in its own way as profoundly Christian as was the man himself. The Christian worldview of The Lord of the Rings is buried much deeper, below the surface, but its roots go down to the foundations of that world in the reflected Logos that drove the language-making mind of its maker. As Shippey puts it, "Tolkien has succeeded in blending suggestions from the optimistic Christian mythology and the tragic Northern one, without impiety to the former or dishonour to the latter."[8] Or, again, he was, like the Gawain poet and the Beowulf poet he had studied so closely, "someone deeply embedded in a Christian and Catholic tradition, but nonetheless . . . ready to make use of the lost, popular, monster-creating 'fairy-tale' traditions which we can infer from his very vocabulary."[9]

One could write whole chapters each on the biblical motifs of creation, fall, redemption, sacrifice, and grace as they permeate the structure, the plot, the texture and flavor of Tolkien's tale. Gandalf, Frodo, and Aragorn are not portraits of Christ the way Aslan is, but they represent the prophet, the suffering Servant, and the coming King in ways that are not accidental. Tolkien did not set out to create Christ figures, but his heroes reflect The Hero in many respects because of the profound ways their maker had absorbed the ways of the Maker in the biblical text.

Tolkien spent his whole life working on the languages and connected mythos out of which The Lord of the Rings grew. He left behind volume upon volume of notes, fragments, and false starts that have since been edited and published for readers hungry for every word of his they can lay their eyes on—thankfully so. But for simplicity's sake, we will limit ourselves in this study to those works that we know he wanted to be published: *The Silmarillion, The Hobbit,* and *The Lord of the Rings.*

Hobbits get no separate mention in *The Silmarillion,* but they should be considered a sub-species of man, one which perhaps has simply not yet been differentiated at that point. "It is plain indeed that in spite of later estrangement hobbits are relatives of ours: far nearer to us than elves or even than dwarves. Of old they spoke the languages of men, after their own fashion, and liked and disliked much the same things as men did. But what exactly our relationship is can no longer be discovered."[10] Man contrasts in many ways with elves and dwarves. But while differing from us in size, hairiness of feet, and adeptness at disappearing, hobbits share our essential nature and hence undoubtedly our destiny.[11] Therefore, for our purposes here, what is said of man applies to hobbit and vice versa.

The Silmarillion gives the background for the mythology and history that lie behind The Lord of the Rings. Though *The Silmarillion* in general is not as polished or well developed as Tolkien's other fiction, it opens with a creation story that is as moving and beautiful as anything he ever wrote. It is also one of the most profound theodicies (explanations of evil and defenses of God's wisdom and goodness in the light of it) ever written. Eru Iluvatar, the One, propounds to the Ainur (roughly equivalent to angels) a theme of music. They enter into it and adumbrate it with harmonies and themes of their own. But Melkor introduces discord into the symphony, trying to wrest the music to his own bombastic purposes. Thus there is war in heaven, until Eru introduces further themes which have the effect of overcoming Melkor's cacophony and actually dovetailing it back into the main composition so that the whole piece ends in a satisfying harmony once again.

"Then Iluvatar spoke, and he said: 'Mighty are the Ainur, and mightiest among them is Melkor; but that he may know, and all the Ainur, that I am Iluvatar, those things that ye have sung, I will show them forth, that ye may see what ye have done. And thou, Melkor, shalt see that no theme may be played that hath not its uttermost source in me, nor can any alter the music in my despite. For he that attempteth this shall prove but mine instrument in the devising of things more wonderful, which he himself hath not imagined."[12]

The symphony is then given reality and becomes the history of the world, Ea. The Ainur enter into it according to their contributions to the music. They have great power and can foresee much because they remember the music, but none sees all, and there are surprises that Iluvatar has reserved for himself. Chief among these, and because related to the later themes of Iluvatar somehow bound up with the redemption of Ea, are the "children of Iluvatar," elves and men.

And [the Ainur] saw with amazement the coming of the Children of Iluvatar, and the habitation that was prepared for them; and they perceived that they themselves in the labour of their music had been busy with the preparation of this dwelling, and yet knew not that it had any purpose beyond its own beauty. For the Children of Iluvatar were conceived by him alone; and they came with the third theme, and were not in the theme which Iluvatar propounded at the beginning, and none of the Ainur had part in their making. Therefore when they beheld them, the more did they love them, being things other than themselves, strange and free, wherein they saw the mind of Iluvatar reflected anew, and learned yet a little more of his wisdom, which otherwise had been hidden even from the Ainur.

Now the Children of Iluvatar are Elves and Men, the Firstborn and the Followers. And amid all the splendours of the World, its vast halls and spaces, and its wheeling fires, Iluvatar chose a place for their habitation in the Deeps of Time and in the midst of the innumerable stars.[13]

The biblical matrix behind Tolkien's world is as essential as it is unobtrusive. The gospel of the salvation of men is something the angels long to look into (1 Pet. 1:12); the manifold wisdom of God will be made known through the church to the principalities and powers in the heavenly places (Eph. 3:10). So in Tolkien's secondary world as well as in God's primary world, one of the functions of man is to reveal something of the wisdom and glory of God to angelic beings. We do this partly because we were unpredictable, a product of his creativity that was not entailed in the laws of physical nature alone. The Ainur are on one level personifications of natural forces: wind, water, fertility, etc. So to say that we came from Iluvatar alone and that they had no part in our making is a symbolic way of repudiating any kind of naturalistic reductionism as an explanation for us.

If we are a mystery to the Ainur, reflecting to them something of the mind of Iluvatar that they would otherwise not have known, we are an even greater mystery to ourselves, wanderers in a world that can tell us clearly only that neither it nor we are self-explanatory. The structure of Tolkien's stories emphasizes the fact that the children of Iluvatar are people on a quest. Whether it is to recover the Silmarils or to destroy the ring or to find the Entwives or just to become the master of Bag End, the children of Iluvatar are always searching for something. And this is especially true of mortal men, by design the ones who are least at home in the world. Tolkien's works are permeated with images that reinforce this view. In one of the most memorable of the songs, we learn that

> The Road goes ever on and on
> Down from the door where it began.
> Now far away the Road has gone
> And I must follow if I can,
> Pursuing it with weary feet
> Until it joins some larger way
> Where many paths and errands meet.
> And whither then? I cannot say.[14]

We see the fires and hear the feasting and revelry in the distance, but we stumble toward them and they disappear. And the sounds of wind and water speak to us in voices we cannot quite hear. "It is said by the Eldar that in water there lives yet the echo of the music of the Ainur more than in any substance else that is in this Earth; and many of the Children of Iluvatar hearken still unsated to the voices of the Sea, and yet know not for what they listen."[15]

This is not a postmodern seeking for its own sake, with no hope of ever finding. But the journey is long, and there are many false trails and byways and no way to make it easy. For it is bound up with the strange nature of our relationship with the physical/temporal world, in it but (unlike the elves) not quite of it. Therefore, Iluvatar "willed that the hearts of Men should seek beyond the world and should find no rest therein; but they should have a virtue to shape their life, amid the powers and chances of the world, beyond the Music of the Ainur, which is as fate to all things else; and of their operation everything should be, in form and deed, completed, and the world fulfilled unto the last and smallest."[16] There is more to man, in other words, than the laws of physics and biochemistry can describe; human beings' emergence into the story had not been predicted in the music of the Ainur, so human beings will never therefore be quite predictable. And our unpredictability is tied to our irreducibility, being made in the image of Iluvatar.

Tolkien interestingly also ties our transcendence of the natural order to that feature of our nature which paradoxically seems most subject to nature: our mortality. "It is one with this gift of freedom that the children of Men dwell only a short space in the world alive, and are not bound to it, and depart soon whither the Elves know not."[17] Though dwarves also have a natural life span, it is we who are explicitly known by the epithet "mortal men." The rhyme of the Rings lists nine for "*Mortal* Men doomed to die."[18] Similar is the old list of creatures kept by the Ents:

Learn now the lore of Living Creatures!
First name the four, the free peoples:
Eldest of all, the elf-children;
Dwarf the delver, dark are his houses;
Ent the earthborn, old as mountains;
Man the mortal, master of horses.[19]

Curiously Tolkien couples our mortality here with one of the features that Chesterton saw as a primary image of our transcendence of the merely natural: the taming of horses. Why this connection? It turns out to be a crucial question, central to the mystery of man indeed. Why are we the only creature able to create noninstinctual relationships with other creatures and also the only one who feels its own mortality to be a mystery?

The elves are immortal within the life of the world. But what might seem a kind of freedom—it certainly seemed so to the Numenoreans, whose envy of it led to their downfall—might turn out in the long run to be rather a limitation. "But the sons of Men die indeed, and leave the world; wherefore they are called the Guests, or the Strangers. Death is their fate, the gift of Iluvatar, which as Time wears even the Powers shall envy. But Melkor has cast his shadow upon it, and confounded it with darkness, and brought forth evil out of good, and fear out of hope. Yet of old the Valar declared to the Elves in Valinor that Men shall join in the Second Music of the Ainur; whereas Iluvatar has not revealed what he purposes for the Elves after the World's end, and Melkor has not discovered it."[20]

Tolkien does not treat our mortality as a result of the Fall so much as a simple datum, a given about us. This is not a departure from the biblical picture. We do not see mankind in *The Silmarillion* in terms of an original pair or a state of innocence, for our origins are hidden in darkness, and we emerge already a race with an unexplained shadow on us from Melkor when the firstborn, the elves, first meet us. If we assume that something like the biblical fall has already happened, then mortality can be seen as a kind of gift, a tourniquet on our spiritual wound or a limit to our slide toward evil. But for Tolkien it is more than that. It is not just that we die; it is that we die *and leave the world*. We are not bound to its circles forever, and he ties this fact to our freedom, our unboundedness, *within* those circles now. We shape our ends beyond the music of the Ainur which is fate to all things else; it is one with this gift of freedom that we live short lives and depart. So in Tolkien's world human mortality becomes a symbol for human irreducibility, for the special relationship that being children of Iluvatar with the gift (or doom) of men gives us to the world. It is the paradoxical limitation that makes freedom possible for good and for ill.[21] This is shown in many ways.

For one thing, the gift of men becomes the occasion for a kind of "second fall" of man. As a reward for their aid in the wars against Melkor, the *Edain*, the most noble of the races of men, are granted a kingdom on the island of Numenor West of the Sea, near to the Blessed Realm where the *Eldar* (elves) live with the Valar, and removed from the strife of Middle Earth. "Thence the Eldar came to the Edain and enriched them with knowledge and many gifts; but one command had been laid upon the Numemoreans, the 'Ban of the Valar': they were forbidden to sail west out of sight of their own shores or to attempt to set foot on the Undying Lands. For though a long span of life had been granted to them, in the beginning thrice that of lesser Men, they must remain mortal, since the Valar were not permitted to take from them the Gift of Men (or the Doom of Men, as it was afterwards called)."[22]

Sauron corrupts their hearts, causing them to envy the immortality in this world enjoyed by the elves. Eventually Ar Pharazon the Golden breaks the ban and assails the Blessed Realm with a great fleet in an attempt to wrest immortality from the Valar (those Ainur who have entered the world as its guardians) by force. They call upon the One, who destroys the fleet in a great upheaval that drowns

Numenor and changes the shape of the world, so that no "straight road" to the West remains except for those elves still wandering in Middle Earth who wish to depart. A faithful remnant of the Edain, faithful to the Valar, flee the wreck of Numenor in nine ships led by Elendil and, washing up on the shores of Middle Earth, found Gondor and Arnor, the Numenorean realms in exile.

An age later their descendants are still the most noble and advanced of men and the most implacable foes of Sauron. But many of them still wrestle with the temptation to become too enamored of this life and hence of trying too hard to prolong it. They build elaborate tombs while the watch on Mordor falters. Ironically, their life span wanes as a result until it is hardly more than that of other men. Mortality is part of human identity though death is not the final word about us. By seeking the wrong kind of immortality in the wrong way, the Numenoreans compromise their humanity, losing that freedom which allows Pippin to cast away his elven brooch in hopes it will help Aragorn to track the orcs who hold him captive. Aragorn approves: he is a slave, he says, who cannot part with a treasure at need.[23] But those who cling too hard to this world and its beauties are destined to see them slip through their fingers anyway. They too will possess only for a time, but they will possess joylessly.

The music of the Ainur is not fate to us because we come from something larger, the third theme of Iluvatar. But the identity of this larger thing is kept mostly in the background, vague and mysterious—even as it is in life. It remains something of a mystery even when we yield to the temptation to overexplain it. Nevertheless, it is there, and it gives the life of man or hobbit who becomes aware of it a sense of purpose. Life is a continuous interaction between the forces of nature, our free and creative selves, influenced but not bound by those forces, and something even larger than either. When those forces of nature seem inevitable or tragic, we call them fate. When they seem rational, we call them the Laws of Science. When they seem fortuitous, we call them luck or chance. They are all really the same thing, and in none of these forms is that thing finally determinative for the children of Iluvatar, ultimately because it is subject to him. That is why prophecies can come true and why our smallness can seem a comfort:

"'Surely you don't disbelieve the prophecies, because you had a hand in bringing them about yourself? You don't really suppose, do you, that all your adventures and escapes were managed by mere luck, just for your sole benefit? You are a very fine person, Mr. Baggins, and I am very fond of you; but you are only quite a little fellow in a wide world after all!'

"'Thank goodness!' said Bilbo laughing, and handed him the tobacco jar."[24]

Life has a meaning because there is Someone big enough to mean it. There is a purpose at work other than our own. Gandalf tells Frodo, "Behind that there was something else at work, beyond any design of the Ring-maker. I can put it no plainer than by saying that Bilbo was *meant* to find the Ring, and *not* by its maker. In which case you also were *meant* to have it. And that may be an encouraging thought."[25]

This larger purpose creates the opportunity for our lives to find meaning in response to it. It is so large that it can easily be confused with fate, but they are not the same, for fate is impersonal, and it makes no difference how we respond to it. The essence of human freedom within the powers of the world, by contrast, is illustrated in Frodo's struggle on Amon Hen. His will seems overpowered both by the call of the Eye of Sauron wanting to find him and a voice commanding him to take off the ring so that Sauron will fail to do so. "The two powers strove in him. For a moment, perfectly balanced between their piercing points, he writhed, tormented. Suddenly he was aware of himself again. Frodo, neither the Voice nor the Eye: free to choose and with one remaining instant in which to do so. He took the Ring off his finger."[26] We find the essence of our humanity, our identity as children of Iluvatar, in those moments when, neither voice nor eye, we show our freedom within the bounds of the world by choosing the right.

Many of us do not make that choice, of course. Gollums and Bill Fernys and Ted Sandymans abound in life. But the choice is always there for us. We are sometimes enabled to make it partly because our creation in God's image makes us irreducible to the forces of mere nature and partly also because it makes us able to grasp something very like Lewis's *Tao*. Eomer complains of the difficulty of the times:

"It is hard to be sure of anything among so many marvels. The world is all grown strange. Elf and Dwarf in company walk in our daily fields; and folk speak with the Lady of the Wood and yet live; and the Sword comes back to war that was broken in the long ages ere the fathers of our fathers rode into the Mark! How shall a man judge what to do in such times?"

"As he ever has judged," said Aragorn. "Good and ill have not changed since yesteryear; nor are they one thing among Elves and Dwarves and another among Men."[27]

Good and evil are eternal principles valid across lines of culture and even species because ultimately they are rooted in the character of One who does not change. Tolkien does not give a running apology for the *Tao* as Lewis does. In a story set in premodern times, he is able simply to assume it. But it is clearly the same conception, equally essential in each of their worlds as part of the definition of who we are.

If life has meaning that flows from choices made with reference to the *Tao*, it must be lived with understanding. One way that understanding comes to us is through stories and legends. We are frequently reminded of the wisdom that is to be found in old tales often known only to old wives, in ways that remind us of Tolkien's defense of Fairy Story in his famous essay. Eomer asks, "'Do we walk in legends or on the green earth in the daylight?'"

"'A man may do both,' said Aragorn. 'For not we but those who come after will make the legends of our time. The green earth, say you? That is a mighty matter of legend, though you tread it under the light of day!'"[28]

Our access to that meaning comes from our rootedness in those stories that tell us who we are. This is something that has to be kept alive deliberately. Ritual is one way of doing that, as we see in a passage that comes as close as Tolkien allows himself to get to portraying the role of religion in Middle Earth.

> Before they ate, Faramir and all his men turned and faced west in a moment of silence. Faramir signed to Frodo and Sam that they should do likewise.
>
> "So we always do," he said, as they sat down: "we look towards Numenor that was, and beyond to Elvenhome that is, and to that which is beyond Elvenhome and will ever be. Have you no such custom at meat?"
>
> "No," said Frodo, feeling strangely rustic and untutored. "But if we are guests, we bow to our host, and after we have eaten we rise and thank him."
>
> "That we do also," said Faramir.[29]

Man's irreducibility to the natural world gives his life its meaning; it also means that there is always the potential for hope. The music of the Ainur is not fate. There can always be surprises, even eucatastrophes, no matter how strong and seemingly irresistible the forces constraining us toward failure or evil may be. After trying to take the Ring, Boromir makes amends and dies at peace, having given his life to defend the hobbits. Even Gollum comes close to repenting on the verge of his betrayal of Frodo and Sam to Shelob, almost caressing Frodo's knee before he is tragically interrupted by

Sam. One of Aragorn's names is Estel, Hope. He is the broken sword reforged, the lost king returning. But perhaps the most moving embodiment of hope is Theoden, who shakes off the poisoned words of Wormtongue, dragging him down to a dotard old age and rises to the occasion of the war in a way that brings a lump into the throat:

> *Out of doubt, out of dark, to the day's rising*
> *he rode singing in the sun, sword unsheathing,*
> *Hope he rekindled, and in hope ended;*
> *over death, over dread, over doom lifted*
> *out of loss, out of life, unto long glory.*[30]

Hope will not die because man is related to the eternal. As Sam sings in his darkest hour,

> *Though here at journey's end I lie*
> *In darkness buried deep,*
> *Beyond all towers strong and high,*
> *Beyond all mountains steep,*
>
> *Above all shadows rides the Sun*
> *And Stars forever dwell:*
> *I will not say the day is done,*
> *Nor bid the stars farewell.*[31]

To be human is to live in hope. Brewer is right to call this "a true and deep perception."[32] But to be human is also to live with the fact that there is no final fruition of that hope in this world, for our destiny lies beyond it. In the tension between those two truths lies the temporal paradox of the works of man, always beginning, always marring, always failing, only to begin again, never achieving for long the greatness that always seems promised but never finally failing at the last or losing sight of that promise either. We live our lives in the shadow of Shelley's Statue of Ozymandias:

> "My name is Ozymandias, king of kings;
> Look on my works, ye mighty, and despair!"

Nothing beside remains. Round the decay
Of that colossal wreck, boundless and bare,
The lone and level sands stretch far away.[33]

A conversation between Legolas and Gimli thus summarizes our history nicely:

"That is a fair lord and a great captain of men," said Legolas. "If Gondor has such men still in these days of fading, great must have been its glory in the days of its rising."

"And doubtless the good stone-work is the older and was wrought in the first building," said Gimli. "It is ever so with the things that Men begin: there is a frost in Spring, or a blight in Summer, and they fail of their promise."

"Yet seldom do they fail of their seed," said Legolas. "And that will lie in the dust and rot to spring up again in times and places unlooked-for. The deeds of Men will outlast us, Gimli."

"And yet come to naught in the end but might-have-beens, I guess," said the Dwarf.

"To that the Elves know not the answer," said Legolas.[34]

The brevity of human life, and hence the bittersweet quality of all that man accomplishes in this life, is brought into sharp relief by the contrast between mortal man and immortal elf. Legolas promises, "In days to come, if my Elven-lord allows, some of our folk shall remove hither; and when we come [Gondor] shall be blessed, for a while. For a while: a month, a life, a hundred years of Men."[35] Our lives in this world are short because this life is not our ultimate end. Nevertheless, we are to love this world for the sake of our Father who made it, not despise it. That is the difficulty of the human condition. We are tempted to take one of the two easier paths: to try to love this life as if it were our final end (like the Numenoreans), that is, to fall into idolatry; or to reject this world and turn from it as cynics always doomed to be disappointed by it. But our true calling is much more difficult: to love it and then to let it go.[36]

Little lettings go, little deaths like Pippin's casting away of the brooch, are practice for the larger one that awaits us all. Frodo's loss of the ability to enjoy the Shire he worked so hard to save is perhaps the most poignant image of this truth. Because it is the preparation for something higher, the letting go is necessary and ultimately blessed when not rejected.[37] But it is seldom easy.

No one understands better the meaning of this doom of men than Aragorn and Arwen, his elvish bride. As the daughter of Elrond Halfelven, she must make an irrevocable choice of which kindred she will belong to. She chooses humanity and mortality for love of Aragorn. "For I am the daughter of Elrond. I shall not go with him now when he departs to the Havens; for mine is the choice of Luthien, and as she so have I chosen, both the sweet and the bitter."[38] Because she has not lived with the doom of men her whole life, its meaning comes to her most potently when the time for Aragorn's departure arrives.

And for all her wisdom and lineage she could not forbear to plead with him to stay yet for a while. She was not yet weary of her days, and thus she tasted the bitterness of the mortality that she had taken upon her. . . . "I say to you, King of the Numenoreans, not till now have I understood the tale of your people and their fall. As wicked fools I scorned them, but I pity them at last. For if this is indeed, as the Eldar say, the gift of the One to Men, it is bitter to receive."

"So it seems," he said. "But let us not be overthrown at the final test, who of old renounced the Shadow and the Ring. In sorrow we must go, but not in despair. Behold! We are not bound for ever to the circles of the world, and beyond them is more than memory. Farewell!"[39]

Beyond the circles of the world is more than memory. And eucatastrophe is the final word about human history for those who can accept it.[40] The Lord of the Rings is "founded on the rock-bottom Christian belief that this world is not our home."[41] And so we learn to live in Middle-Earth as true men and women, and to leave it as Gandalf teaches us: "Well, here at last, dear friends, on the shores of the Sea comes the end of our fellowship in Middle-Earth. Go in peace! I will not say: do not weep; for not all tears are an evil."[42]

COMMENTARY, GENESIS 2:19, NO. 2

Sonnet XXXVII

And how he thought about them, trooping past,
  Stooping to lick his hand or sniff his knee—
  Tiny as bee or hummingbird, or vast
  In girth the river-horse—and first to see
In fur and feather, clad heraldically,
  The colors—and the antics!—speechless, stare
  At scampering mice, at stallions' thunder, tree-
  Like limbs of elephants, ambling bulk of bear—
This creativity beyond compare—
  What fruit brought forth in bare but fertile mind;
  From sound and sight, throat muscles, subtle air
  To weave the words, the Poet's power unbind:
To call the Correspondences by name
  As Adam called the animals who came.

—D.T.W.

CONCLUSION

*"There's a divinity that shapes our ends,
Roughhew them how we will."*

—SHAKESPEARE, *HAMLET*

IS MAN A MYTH? Does the traditional Christian concept of humanity describe a reality that exists? Are we that great and true amphibium of Sir Thomas Browne, designed to live simultaneously in the diverse and distinguished worlds of spirit and matter as indeed the crucial bridge between them? Or are we completely describable in materialistic or naturalistic terms? Are we made in the image of God? Or is he just a projection of our own image onto a cosmic screen? Are we rational beings capable of being enlightened by a principle of universal reason? Or are we just bundles of biophysical impulses capable of rationalization? Three great Christian thinkers of the recent past help to bring clarity to these questions, showing us both the richness of the Christian picture of humanity and the elegance of its fit with our full experience of life, when we do not allow that fullness to be truncated by a preempting reductionism.

Chesterton found two things inexplicable on a materialistic basis: the creature called man and the man called Christ, neither of which would consent to being reduced to mere nature. Art, he said, is the

132

signature of man, and it signs a mind that transcends the merely natural, demanding that we look at the world in terms of the philosophy
of stories, with the greatest story ever told (not the history of cows in
twelve volumes) as the key to the meaning of it all.

Lewis explicated the ethical implications of our irreducibility
to mere nature in the nonmaterial *Tao*, rebellion against which in
the name of reductionist philosophies threatens our humanity. He
imaginatively shows us that *Tao* at work, on other planets and in a
version of our own world in the planetary mythology of The Space
Trilogy and in a purely imaginary land in The Chronicles of Narnia.
In the Trilogy he identifies and names the category we belong to.
We are hnau, rational/spiritual physical creatures. By comparing and
contrasting us with other hnau there and with talking beasts in the
Chronicles, he shows us a portrait of ourselves as copies of Maleldil,
with the horrors and the splendors of what we were, what we have
become, what we might have been, and what we shall be in the Great
Dance.

Tolkien brings us full circle, explaining even more fully why
storytelling is central to this irreducible human nature, and finding
the fulfillment of our most moving stories in the story of Christ, that
point where, as Lewis (who learned it from him) would put it, myth
entered history. In mythological images informed by this Christian
philosophy, he shows us what it means to be children of Iluvatar, who
came with the Third Theme and are mortal but also and thereby not
bound to the circles of the world. Mortal man is a creature whose
origins keep him ever from finally abandoning freedom, meaning,
and hope, even as they also prevent his ever finding them finally in
this world. This is the bittersweet leaven that permeates all our most
moving stories.

These three men lived and wrote with a wholeness of vision that
increasingly eludes us[1] partly because, with all their flaws and faults,
they were working from a model of humanity still unfragmented,

still stubbornly untruncated by the reductionism that increasingly surrounded them and of whose consequences they warned so forcefully. What Patrick says of Lewis was true of all of them: "In his work metaphysics lived; history found significant unity; and reason joined imagination."[2] This wholeness, with its near synonym *integration,* was possible because for them body and spirit, history and myth, imagination and reason all found their unity, as indeed all of reality does, in the creative and incarnated Logos which is also the ultimate paradigm of humanity, the "Son of Man": the person of Jesus Christ. Thus they enable us to do what Harold O. J. Brown says is needed for the preservation of our civilization: "What is necessary is to remember or learn for the first time that we are not blind products of time plus space plus chance, but we have a dignity that comes from God."[3]

So the human race still hangs on. In spite of every attempt to define it out of existence, it keeps building its unbirdlike nests and writing its unbovine histories. Perhaps if we could read the faun's-eye view of our race that Lucy saw in Mr. Tumnus's library, we should find the answer to its titular question laden with Chestertonian irony. Is man a myth? It depends on what we mean. Man, the spiritual animal whose mind transcends the physically quantifiable in ways that are of mythic proportions, is not a myth (in the sense that he does not exist), though he is both *mythopoeic* and *mythopathic.* But man, the product of evolution who can be explained fully in terms of material and mechanical processes, is definitely a myth, a myth created by man the mythmaker. For this man is a story that attempts to explain the world and explains it well as long as we do not step outside the limited vision of reductionist materialism. But there are older myths, more redolent of the full truth about us if not more powerful to shape our conceptions. And one of those, if these men were right, is the true myth, the one story that really does explain the world.

THE SAINTS BELIEVE WHAT EVERY LOVER KNOWS

Villanelle No. 7

The saints believe what every lover knows
   Who, gazing on one face, can plainly see
   The glory latent in the flesh, a rose.
If love is what leads lovers to compose
   Their songs of praise and deeds of charity,
   Then saints believe what every lover knows.
The truth the heavens declare, the firmament shows,
   To starry-eyed and moonstruck is most free:
   The glory latent. In the flesh, a rose
Can shine in cheeks as brightly, and disclose
   To opened eyes as deep a mystery,
   Which saints believe and every lover knows.
Yet ash to ash and dust to dust it goes,
   An aching void its only legacy,
   The glory latent in the flesh. A rose

Will lose its petals, yet the spring bestows
New life; but what hope for the flesh can be?
The saints believe what every lover knows:
The Glory latent in the Flesh arose.

—D.T.W.

Appendix A

STORIES AND STOCK RESPONSES

C. S. Lewis on Christianity and Literature

"Now, good Cesario, but that piece of song,
That old and antique song we heard last night,
Methought it did relieve my passion much,
More than light airs and recollected terms
Of these most brisk and giddy-paced times."

—DUKE ORSINO OF ILLYRICA, IN SHAKESPEARE'S
THE MERCHANT OF VENICE

BECAUSE "MAN AS STORYTELLER" is one of the central elements in Chesterton's "philosophy of stories" as fleshed out by Tolkien, because it has played such a central role in our development of the mere Christian view of human nature in this study, and because most of Lewis's many treatments of this idea lie outside those books in which he gives direct attention to anthropology, i.e. the ones we have given our attention to here, it seems useful to include a short look at Lewis's views on the nature of literature and its place in the Christian life.

C. S. Lewis is often underappreciated as a literary theorist. He was a historian of literature whose analyses are still indispensable to students of the Middle Ages and the Renaissance half a century later; he created a great deal of superb literature himself, in both fiction and nonfiction; and he was also the author of a number of works that deal directly with the nature and value of the products of the mind and a fruitful approach to them, from books like *An Experiment in Criticism* and *The Abolition of Man* to the numerous essays buried in various collections. But most of his scholarly writing on literature comes to us in the guise of practical criticism (*A Preface to Paradise Lost*) or literary history (*OHEL, The Allegory of Love,* and similar words). Nevertheless, all these writings are informed by a unified approach that has been influential, especially among Christian believers. No thinker has done more to help evangelical Christians relate their Christian faith to culture, especially literary culture, than C. S. Lewis.

Work on various aspects of Lewis's thinking about literature has been done by scholars such as Bruce Edwards, Charles Huttar, Robert Stock, Peter Schakel, and Stephen Thorson, *inter alia.* With the exception of Edwards, they have tended to focus on only one aspect of his approach at a time. But while Edwards's fine book *A Rhetoric of Reading: C. S. Lewis's Defense of Western Literacy* is more comprehensive, its focus is how Lewis's thinking impacts literary critics. This essay looks at what Lewis has to say to us, not as critics or scholars primarily, but as readers. Or, to put it another way, Edwards studied Lewis's views on critical theory, on *how* to read; this essay will deal more with the question of the insights Lewis's literary theory provides on *why* we read and what we can get out of it.

The impressively integrated unity of Lewis's thinking on many topics makes it easy to miss the fact that he did mature as a Christian thinker through the years. It is easy to understand how Smith could say that Lewis's thought "appeared almost full blown in the earliest Christian writings that came from his pen"[1] so that one can ignore chronological position in the Lewis corpus without distorting his thinking, for indeed this is generally so. But, as Schakel has pointed out, this generalization is not always true and therefore needs to be demonstrated on any given point rather than merely assumed.[2] In this essay we will try to notice Lewis's growth while exhibiting the unity of his thinking as we pull together the many comments on the nature and purpose of reading in the Christian life that Lewis left scattered throughout his broad corpus of critical writing.

The Legitimacy of Literature

Naturally, but unfortunately, people looking to Lewis for guidance in these matters often begin (and often end) at an essay with the obvious title of "Christianity and Culture" (originally published in 1940), without realizing that significant development took place in Lewis's thought as expressed in later essays. Superficial readings of that piece have even given rise to the strange notion that Lewis had an "anti-cultural bias."[3] After all, Lewis does say that "I think we can still believe culture to be innocent after we have read the New Testament; I cannot see that we are encouraged to think it important."[4] The glory of God is "the real business of life," and the salvation of souls is "our *only* means to glorifying Him" (emphasis added).[5] And he adds in another essay from about the same time that "the Christian knows from the outset that the salvation of a single soul is more important than the production or preservation of all the epics and tragedies in the world."[6] Lewis would maintain his high view of the value of the salvation of a single soul[7]—but as the *only* means of glorifying God? Later essays would show an increase in balance and maturity in his views on these topics as well as continuity with the positions taken earlier.

Actually, in "Christianity and Culture," Lewis was making the point that idolization of culture (including literature) corrupts and destroys culture. He was reacting against the tendency of critics like Matthew Arnold to make culture a substitute for religion.[8] Just as "those who make religion their God will not have God for their religion,"[9] so those who make culture their God will enjoy neither a relationship with God nor good literature. It was a point he would make more clearly and forcefully again later (1955) in an essay entitled "Lilies that Fester." When sophistication is valued for its own sake rather than because it can get us closer to the goodness, truth, or beauty in the text and students are expected to feign it in order to be considered educated, it actually becomes a barrier between us and that goodness, truth, or beauty, driving the true, spontaneous, and natural appreciation of literature underground while it feeds on purely specious grounds our pride. Just as theocracy is the worst form of government because it ironically destroys genuine religion, "charientocracy," the rule of the artificially "cultured," is inimical to all the goods that culture can really give.

In "Christianity and Culture," then, Lewis was engaged in the task of defending the *innocence* of literary pursuits. He offers four arguments in support of this conclusion. First, literary pursuits may be a way of making one's living. If John the Baptist told even soldiers and tax collectors to follow the moral law and then "sent them back to their jobs,"[10] then surely a Christian may be a writer or a critic. Second, it is better that Christians participate in culture as salt and light than to abandon it to the enemy completely. They would be an "antidote" to the abuse of culture not by disguising homiletics and apologetics as culture but simply by doing good and wholesome work.[11] Third, culture gives pleasure, which is a good thing in itself. Pleasure is good, and sin is accepting that good "under conditions that imply a breach of the moral law."[12] When the pleasures of culture do not violate those conditions, we may "enjoy them ourselves, and lawfully, even charitably, teach others to enjoy them."[13] Fourth, culture is a repository of the best natural or "sub-Christian" values, which, while not of saving significance, are not therefore to be despised; it can be for some a *praeparatio evangelium* (preparation for the gospel), for "any road out of Jerusalem may also be a road into Jerusalem."[14]

So far, so good; but in later essays Lewis would go on to develop much more fully not just the innocence but also the positive values of literary culture. Thorson points out the fact that Lewis himself was a person who had received the benefit of the *praeparatio evangelium* from his own reading of imaginative literature.[15] Perhaps it was this fact which led Lewis to go beyond his defense of culture's potential innocence in "Christianity and Culture" to articulate the much more positive view outlined below.

A Larger World

In the first place, literature enlarges our world of experience to include both more of the physical world and things not yet imagined, giving the actual world a "new dimension of depth."[16] Poetic language can express "experience which is not available to us in normal life at all" by using "factors within our experience so that they become pointers to something outside our experience."[17] None of us, for example, has experienced apotheosis. But Shelley gives us an idea what it might be like with his line, "My soul is an enchanted boat." Lewis insists that this is much more than just a fancy way of saying, "Gee! This is fine."[18] An enchanted boat would move effortlessly, without propulsion, to its intended destination. Because we have experienced boats which require wind, oar, or steam, we can imagine one that would not and transfer this image by analogy to the soul, which could then be imagined as freed from its current weights and entanglements to reach unimpeded its ends: enlightenment, integration, communion, etc.

I personally have never slain a dragon or met an elf (at least, not for certain). I have not visited another planet, led a charge on horseback, or lived in the Middle Ages. Yet I know something of what these experiences might be like. Is this knowledge gained from literature mere illusion? Definitely not. There was a time I had not visited England but only read about it, more in books of fiction than of information. When I got there, there were surprises in store for me of course, but there was also much that was already familiar. Direct experience made small adjustments to and augmentations of my "literary" knowledge of the real England gained through vicarious experience of imagined ones, but it did not overturn it. When we experience this kind of confirmation often enough and in various ways, we learn to trust the inner consistency of reality projected by a well-constructed story to give us something significant, an exploration of the potentialities of human experience of worlds actual or imagined that can ring true to reality. Literal truth is not the only kind we know or need.

The effect of this kind of reading is what Lewis called "the enormous extension of our being which we owe to authors." An unliterary person "may be full of goodness and good sense, but he inhabits a tiny world." This suffocating narrowness, the provincialism of being shut up to one's own direct experience, literature can help us avoid. "My own eyes are not enough for me," Lewis avers; "I would see through those of others."[19] He even wishes that animals could write books so that we could see through their eyes. And what one sees thus can be broadening and deepening indeed:

> Strangeness that moves us more than fear,
> Beauty that stabs with tingling spear,
> Or Wonder, laying on one's heart

That finger-tip at which we start
As if some thought too swift and shy
For reason's grasp had just gone by.[20]

A Baptized Imagination

In the second place, this expansion of horizons makes it possible for literature to strip Christian doctrines of their "stained glass and Sunday School associations" and allow them to appear in their "real potency,"[21] a possibility Lewis himself magnificently realized in the Narnia books and the Space Trilogy. Why did the story of a dying God which repelled the young Lewis in the Gospels move him so deeply when he met it in pagan mythology? Partly because his guard was down when reading mythology, but just as much because of the expansion of our grasp of the potentialities of reality that we have already seen literature can give us. The sober historicity of the Gospels is valuable in one way, the imaginative realizations of literary treatments in another. So Lewis's imagination was "baptized" by reading George MacDonald's *Phantastes* and *Lillith* before his actual conversion.[22]

This baptism of the imagination, which allows us to see Christian truths more clearly and deeply when we meet them in the Bible, can happen in two ways: first, by encountering similar or parallel ideas imaginatively fleshed out in non-Christian literature (e.g., Lewis's encounters with the dying god in pagan myth), and second, by seeing newly minted images created as deliberate incarnations of Christian ideas (e.g., Lewis's experience of "the holy" in MacDonald). In the first case, parallel with the idea of culture as a repository of the best "sub-Christian" ideals in "Christianity and Culture" but going beyond it, literature can contain something like the "spilled religion" Lewis had seen in Romanticism as early as 1933. Lewis never compromises the sub-Christian nature of what one sees there. A person who has religion "ought not to spill it." But what if one who does not have it finds it in such a messy state? "Does it follow that he who finds it spilled should avert his eyes? How if there is a man to whom these bright drops on the floor are the beginning of a trail which, duly followed, will lead him in the end to taste the cup itself?"[23] Lewis was of course himself a man who, under Tolkien's influence, had so followed and so drunk.

Having drunk deeply both of pagan myth and Christian retelling, Lewis also became himself a master of the second way. We have seen the cross a thousand times and may be either bored with it or hostile to it, but the Stone Table of Narnia sneaks up on us and gets under our skins, sending us back to the cross with eyes newly opened. When we read Genesis, we Christians may get bogged down in the necessary tasks of defending the text against fragmentation from the purveyors of the Documentary Hypothesis or dismissal from adherents of the theory of Naturalistic Evolution. But when we watch the Green Lady of Perelandra debating the Unman with the future of her still innocent race at stake, the more important issues of the other text become real to us both afresh and in new ways. Her floating islands are not just an interesting feature of a fantasy landscape but along with the fixed land and the coming waves become rich and powerful natural symbols for the spiritual issues of trust and obedience.[24]

What is the result? Just as Maleldil makes Tinidril "older" through Ransom's arrival, the same thing can happen to us as readers. Schakel describes this making older as having happened to Lewis himself when reading MacDonald: "When imagination as spiritual experience encountered the true divine Spirit, in the quality of Holiness, a transformation was initiated."[25] As Aslan tells Edmund and Lucy, in their world he has another name. "You must learn to know me by that name. This was the very reason why you were brought to Narnia, that by knowing me here for a little, you may know me better there."[26] Truly Shaw's description of Lewis's achievement is justified: "He folded time and eternity into folios, condensed a radiance ready to bear a weight of glory."[27]

Good "Stock" Responses

In the third place, literature can have some of the significance Lewis seemed to deny it in "Christianity and Culture" through the creation of positive role models and the reinforcement of healthy "stock responses." Lewis had little sympathy with the criticism of I. A. Richards and the early T. S. Eliot, influential in his time, which emphasized the importance of a finely tuned sensibility in literary taste, denigrating what were seen as crude and traditional "stock responses" as opposed to the preferred "direct free play of experience."[28] (No doubt this "direct free play of experience" was a precursor of the "free play of the mind in the text" valued by postmodern reader-centered critics; but that is another story.) Eliot, for example, saw the mind of the mature poet as "a finely perfected medium in which special, or varied feelings are at liberty to enter into new combinations"[29] and valued literature for the ways in which it produces "new variations of sensibility."[30] Lewis thought this emphasis could lead only to the kind of corrupting decadence and false sophistication he warned against in "Lilies that Fester" and saw Eliot's early poetry as proof that his concerns were valid. (Lewis never publicly responded to the poetry Eliot wrote later, after his conversion, which seems less deliberately and unnecessarily obscure; we can only speculate that he might have viewed it differently.) In a famous jab at "The Love Song of J. Alfred Prufrock," Lewis's *persona* claims to be

> So coarse, the things that poets see
> Are obstinately invisible to me.
> For twenty years, I've stared my level best

To see if evening—any evening—would suggest
A patient etherized upon a table;
In vain. I simply wasn't able.[31]

Huttar elucidates the sophistication of Lewis's commentary, doubting that he actually misunderstood Eliot so far as to think the etherized patient was intended as a description of the sky rather than as a portrait of Prufrock's sensibility, and suggesting that Lewis might have been objecting to "a widespread attitude which he finds objectionable," which the passage from "Prufrock" illustrates rather than exemplifies.[32] His reading is interesting and possible, but he also rightly notes that it does not affect the "serious point" being made about language and morals.[33] Whether the problem is in Prufrock or in Eliot, there is something troubling about what seemed to be a growing taste for the kind of imagery Lewis was satirizing.

In contrast, Lewis saw the great literature of the past as a repository of cultural memory and wisdom that could help us rightly order our response to the world in terms of healthy and appropriate stock responses: love is sweet, death is bitter, virtue is lovely, children or gardens are delightful. Instead of the newer, more "sophisticated" images, it was full of

Dull things . . . peacocks, honey, the Great Wall, Aldebaran,
Silver weirs, new-cut grass, wave on the beach, hard gem,
The shapes of horse and woman, Athens, Troy, Jerusalem.[34]

There is more at stake here than simply our taste in imagery. The emphasis on sophisticated sensibility as a sufficient end in itself was consistent with the antididactic bent of modern criticism, and Lewis's objections to this aestheticism were consonant with his defense of the older tradition in which the purpose of literature is "to delight and to teach." The function of the poet for Lewis then is not so much the relatively trivial one of expressing ever finer shades of sensibility but the grand one of transmitting the form of virtue received from the past. Virtue is not so much a finely as a *rightly* organized response of the whole person, including understanding, emotion, and will. "In rhetoric imagination is present for the sake of passion (and therefore in the long run for the sake of action), while in poetry passion is present for the sake of imagination and therefore, in the long run, for the sake of wisdom or spiritual health—the rightness and richness of a man's total response to the world."[35]

The Eliotian and Ricardian emphasis on sophisticated sensibility as a sufficient end in itself was also consistent with what Huttar calls the "truncated sense of what is real"[36] that Lewis opposed in works like *Miracles* and *The Abolition of Man*. Richards thought there were only two kinds of language: "scientific" language, which conveys information, and "emotive" language, which conveys the emotional attitude of the speaker but tells us nothing about its apparent reference.[37] It sounds exactly like the view of Gaius and Titius that Lewis had attacked in *The Abolition of Man* (see chapter 2)—that when someone tells you that a waterfall is sublime, he appears "to be making a remark about the waterfall. . . . Actually . . . he was not making a remark about a waterfall at all, but a remark about his own feelings."[38] If this view is accepted, it follows that poetry, which is quintessentially "emotive" language, has no referent in the external world. All it can communicate is sensibility, the inner life of the speaker. But Lewis believed that the values embodied in what he called the *Tao* have their own kind of objective reality. If sublimity could not be a real attribute of a waterfall, then neither could goodness be a real attribute of an action or of a virtue, or evil a real attribute of an action or a vice.[39] The modernist metaphysic—its denial of reality to anything other than atoms in motion—entails a view of literature that reduces to aestheticism, an emphasis on sophisticated emotional responses as ends in themselves. Lewis clearly saw the connection between metaphysics and literary theory and realized that to oppose the one view logically requires one to oppose the other.

Therefore, the predominance in literature of traditional themes embodied imaginatively in traditional forms was not for Lewis an issue merely of aesthetics and sensibility but of cultural life and death. "Poetry was formerly one of the chief means whereby each generation learned to copy, and by copying to make the good Stock Responses. Since poetry has abandoned that office, the world has not bettered."[40] Hence, "Since it is likely that [children] will meet cruel enemies, let them at least have heard of brave knights and heroic courage."[41] And Lewis would probably add if he were alive today, let them not all be filtered through the lens of postmodern ironic cynicism.

A Cure for Chronological Snobbery

Finally, literature can cure our chronological snobbery and provincialism and fortify us in the "mere Christianity" that has remained constant through the ages. The modern age was prone to think that its advances in science and technology made it superior to previous eras, to feel it could smugly ignore the wisdom of the past. T. S. Eliot (ironically, given Lewis's antipathy to his criticism) recognized this modernist propensity and gave a classic response to it: "Someone said: 'The dead writers are remote from us because we *know* so much more than they did.' Precisely, and they are that which we know."[42] Postmodernism has this tendency in an even more pronounced form, reducing what past ages presented as attempts at rational thought to mere rhetoric and viewing all truth claims with profound suspicion. The only thing it does not seem to question is its own assumed superior standpoint that allows it to question everything else.

Lewis credited Owen Barfield with "destroying forever" in Lewis's own mind this "'chronological snobbery,' the uncritical acceptance of the intellectual climate common to our own age and the assumption that whatever has gone out of date is on that account discredited."[43] Lewis summarizes Barfield's argument thus: "You must find out why it went out of date. Was it ever refuted (and if so by whom, where, and how conclusively) or did it merely die away as fashions do? If the latter, this tells us nothing about its truth or falsehood. From seeing this, one passes to the realization that our own age is also 'a period,' and certainly has, like all periods, its own characteristic illusions. They are likeliest to lurk in those widespread assumptions which are so ingrained in the age that no one dares to attack or feels it necessary to defend them."[44]

The reduction of our own age to the status of a "period" with its own illusions bears a surface resemblance to some postmodern analyses which also rightly refuse to "privilege" modern points of view, "situating" all truth claims as mere expressions of their time and place. But there is a major difference. Postmodernist nihilism disallows any legitimate truth claims and thus dissolves our own claims to enlightenment, finding the modern age as benighted (if not more so) as any other. Lewis, instead of lowering our own age to the level of the benighted past, finds previous ages as potentially enlightened (and therefore enlightening) as our own, though at different points. He is able to do this because for him and Barfield warranted belief was still theoretically possible, making questions like "Who refuted it? When? How?" relevant. Many postmodern versions of the attack on chronological snobbery are therefore stultifying, ultimately making progress toward enlightenment impossible. Lewis and Barfield, on the other hand, are liberating, freeing us from the shackles of our own limitations to learn without prejudice from the wisdom of the ages.

This rejection of chronological snobbery became a cornerstone of Lewis's own thinking that informs his popular apologetics as well as his literary criticism and was a source of much of their strength. He made a classic application of it to our reading in his famous essay "On the Reading of Old Books." Every age, he noted, makes its own errors. Those of the past are at least different from ours and mostly have already been seen through. They are thus not a danger to us and are not likely uncritically to reinforce our own mistakes. Those readers who are exposed only to the spirit of the age in which they live have no protection against its errors. But those who live with the literature of the past discover a place to stand that gives them some critical distance from their own period, and more: "a standard of plain, central Christianity ('mere Christianity' as Baxter called it) which puts the controversies of the moment in their proper perspective."[45] Therefore, to avoid becoming captives of the spirit of the age, we must "keep the clean sea breeze of the centuries blowing through our minds"[46] by reading old books. (The books of the future would achieve the same end but are unfortunately not available.) As with St. Athanasius, who clung to Trinitarian orthodoxy when it was unfashionable to do so, it is the glory of these old books that they did not move with the times, and their reward is that they therefore remain for all time.

Summary

In Lewis's mature thinking, then, the study of literature is not only innocent but essential to a full and rich life, particularly a full and rich Christian life. While he remained adamantly opposed to aestheticism or to any notion that becoming more cultured necessarily makes one a better person ("Lilies that Fester"), he explored a number of ways in which culture, particularly literature, can contribute to a good life well lived to the glory of God. Thorson captures the balance nicely: "Although Lewis refused to call aesthetic and imaginative experiences spiritual, he did not empty them of spiritual significance."[47] Literature can expand the horizons of and deepen our capacity for experience; it can open our eyes to Christian truths which might otherwise have escaped us or had less impact had we read only the Bible; it can transmit and reinforce the collective experience and wisdom of human civilization; and it can be the great antidote to the spirit of the age. But it does not confer these benefits automatically, *ex opere operato*; if we read as aesthetes rather than humble receivers of the author's intent or as self-conscious pursuers of culture rather than seekers of truth, it can have the opposite effect and be a horribly corrupting influence.[48]

If Lewis was right, few things could be more crucial to the health of a culture—or to the health of the church within that culture—than having a love for and a sound approach to literature. As the academic study of literature as a discipline has become more ideologically bound and politicized than ever, his voice desperately needs to be heard again, like a John the Baptist crying in the wilderness and calling us back to sanity.[49] And with these matters, readers of any religious persuasion, but especially those who share Lewis's Christian worldview, must be concerned.

THE LOGIC OF POSTMODERNISM

Villanelle No. 26

"Logic's nothing but a verbal trick,"
Postmodern thinkers often like to claim.
They work quite hard to make that judgment stick.
All those who don't agree are simply thick,
Incompetent to play the language game
Where logic's nothing but a verbal trick.
It's all a plot by dead white males to kick
Non-Westerners and keep them meek and tame?
Well, that's one way to make their judgment stick.
"Is there a Text in this class?" Don't be quick
To ask if there's a prof to ask the same,
For logic's nothing but a verbal trick.
All truth is surreptitious rhetoric,
For words call only other words by name;
The will to power makes this judgment stick!
You say it all sounds just a bit too slick?
Shh! Shh! Don't give the scam away—for shame!
If logic's nothing but a verbal trick,
What logic then can make this judgment stick?

—D.T.W.

Appendix B

THE GREAT DIVIDE

The Church and the
Postmodernist Challenge

Taffeta phrases, silken terms precise,
Three-piled hyperboles, spruce affectation,
Figures pedantical—these summer flies
Have blown me full of maggot ostentation.

—BEROWNE, IN SHAKESPEARE'S *LOVE'S LABOR'S LOST*

WE HAVE HAD OCCASION to say a fair bit about postmodernism in these pages. Because it is a large and confusing topic in its own right and because it constitutes in many ways a more radical challenge to the traditional Christian view of man even than modernism did, it seems worthwhile to give it some special attention in an appendix. What exactly is it, where does it come from, and how best might we respond to it?

The church of Jesus Christ today faces a challenge far greater than the Renaissance, more potentially divisive than the Reformation,

153

more insidious in its inroads into the life of the church itself than the secularist rationalism of the "Endarkenment."

If my words sound alarmist, well, I am alarmed. As one who is both a college professor and a pastor, I have had the opportunity to watch this new threat growing in the academy, and I now see it becoming planted firmly in the lives of Christian young people who subjectively love Jesus, go to Bible studies, and sing all the right choruses. But their minds are increasingly structured and controlled by paradigms which are in deadly conflict with the Christian world-view and the Christian tradition as any of us—Protestant, Catholic, or Orthodox, Reformed, Dispensationalist, or Arminian—have ever understood it. And they are blithely unaware of the contradiction. Indeed, pointing out that it *is* a contradiction is likely to have little meaning to them.

What is at stake is not just Christian truth but whether any assertion can be described as true; in other words, not just the Christian message but the framework of shared experience and categories that makes possible any communication at all between the church and its members or the church and the world it was sent to reach. And so, let me describe this new way of thinking, inimical not only to the Christian faith but to anything we have ever recognized as rational thought in the West. Since the academy is still the primary spring from which it flows, I shall describe it as I have encountered it there. For it is important, not simply that we reject and condemn it but that first we understand it so we can reject it and minister to those bamboozled by it, with understanding.

The Christian professor's life is full of challenges. Many of our students come to us like Robert Frost's farmer-neighbor in "Mending Wall." They will not go behind their fathers' sayings but like having thought of them so well that they say them again: "Good fences make good neighbors." Spring is the mischief in their professors, who want to put an idea in their heads: "Why do they make good neighbors?" But a certain type of professor, often oxymoronically styled "postmodernist," wants to go further: to question not only why they make good neighbors or even whether they make good neighbors (which might be a question worth asking) but whether they are not such arbitrary social constructs that the ability to distinguish one neighbor from another, or a good one from a bad, breaks down completely. Something there is that doesn't love a wall. But this gives their more traditional colleagues pause. For they fear that, when all fences have been knocked down thus, civilization will have been destroyed, and the Goths and Vandals will come again.

Labels are convenient but problematic, a mixed good or a necessary evil. By *postmodernist* here I do not mean all people who have adopted that label or had it applied to them. I am not defending modernism or implying that having gotten beyond it is necessarily bad. Christians were pointing out the limitations of the Modernist Project (the attempt, since the Enlightenment, to subsume all reality and all knowledge under the rubric of rationalistic scientific objectivity) long before it was fashionable to do so. But they did not do so by throwing the rational baby out with the rationalist bathwater. If we are going to leave one error behind, it behooves us not to exchange it for a worse.

Postmodernism, as I shall use the term here, means precisely that style of disillusionment with modernity which is too sophisticated to be able to make any clear distinction between babies and bathwater because it rejects all distinctions as arbitrary impositions upon a reality too complex to be categorized. Angry at itself for having trusted in scientific rationality's promise to deliver absolute truth with absolute objectivity, it now cynically rejects all truth claims as equally empty promises. Once burned and twice shy, it starts from the conviction that anyone peddling truth claims is selling snake oil. Believing that truth is an illusion, it sees all attempts at analysis or even definition as thin disguises for the imposition of power. Therefore it manifests itself in literary study that ignores (or "deconstructs") traditional issues of meaning or even aesthetics and concentrates instead on the ways that texts advance the agendas of various groups, usually defined in terms of race, class, or gender. I shall contrast it here not with modernism but with something far older that I will call "The Tradition."

Not every scholar who has looked at race or gender issues in literature will be fairly represented by the following characterizations. But neither do I mean only the hard-core followers of postmodernist thinkers such as Jacques Derrida or Stanley Fish; rather, I refer also to the host of scholars (and their students, including Christian students) who have adopted their methods without necessarily thinking through their epistemological and ethical implications but whose analyses are nonetheless affected by them.

Neither by *traditionalist* do I mean every redneck or robber-baron capitalist who ever gave the phrase "ugly American" its meaning. But there is a tradition that holds together thinkers as diverse as Socrates, Erasmus, Aquinas, and the great Protestant Reformers, Edmund Burke and Dr. Johnson, Thomas Jefferson and Russell Kirk, C. S. Lewis and T. S. Eliot, Dorothy L. Sayers and Flannery O'Connor, which makes them all, in spite of their differences, part of a single conversation taking place in the same universe of discourse. Some of these people found themselves on different sides of some fences (some were outside the church), but they were still able to cooperate in examining and repairing them, to each the boulders that had fallen to each. They differ from the type of postmodernist thinker I am describing by believing that, while the usefulness or proper location of any given fence might be an open question, there *is* a difference between one field and another rather than an endlessly open play of French-accented *différance*; and, hence, in not wanting to tear down all the fences they inherited from their ancestors so they can start over again from scratch.

Questioning, to both groups, is an intellectual good. By it the mixture of truth and error, gold and dross, that constitutes our thoughts is refined. But for the traditionalist, questioning is not an end in itself. It has value in so far as purer gold is desirable. But if we question whether gold is really more precious than lead, the process of refinement grinds to a halt, and our intellectual currency becomes debased. When questioning becomes an end in itself, no longer limited either by first principles (which the postmodernist thinks are just arbitrary social conventions) or facts (which she thinks are endlessly receding, unfixable, and arbitrarily selected bits of experience), then not one stone is left upon a stone. When the mind becomes its own place, which in itself can make a heaven of hell, a hell of heaven, then indeed Frost's apples do get over and eat the cones under his neighbor's pines. Then we do not even have the dignity of living in such an ordered and civilized place as the hell in which Milton's Satan makes such exalted claims for his mind; for chaos has come again.

The believing church, as the most forthright denier that the mind is its own place and the strongest contender for the existence of an objective truth outside the mind, bears the brunt of the attack, but what is under attack is something even more basic: the legitimacy of the larger human conversation of which the church has been a part. What is questioned is *anyone's* right to assert that *anything* is true. Nay, more than questioned: any "totalizing" or "centering" discourse, that is, any claim to have a viewpoint that is more than blatantly rationalized self-interest, is denied as illegitimate at the outset.

This is more than the old modernist relativism: truth is not merely denied as *illusory*, as in late relativist modernism; it is now redefined as *evil*. Truth for the postmodernist is and can be nothing more than a disguise for the exercise of raw power. Only an ironic infinite, regress of questions, never leading to answers, is allowed. One therefore questions everything and affirms nothing except that all affirmations are illegitimate. This is really the ultimate form of intellectual rebellion against authority, especially the authority of God. Therefore, Christian civilization in general and the church in particular are singled out for special attention in the application of this intellectual acid that eats away at the foundations of all claims to truth, meaning, and authority.

Hence, one of the things that postmodernist scholars love to question is the unique value, the superiority, and hence the authority of our Western, Greco-Roman, Judaeo-Christian civilization. They question the legitimacy of giving its history, its philosophy, its literary canon a "privileged" place in the academy. We have traditionally viewed this civilization as the result of a providential blending of elements from Greek, Roman, Hebrew, and Christian sources that produced a unique and precious set of values: the primacy of truth, the rule of law rather than of men, the worth of the individual and his or her liberty, freedom of speech and religion, democracy—treasures which have arisen and been sustainable only in those societies nurtured by this tradition. Their seeds were planted at least as early as Plato's "Apology of Socrates" and found in Christendom the providentially prepared soil in which alone they could truly flourish. They emerged only gradually even there and never perfectly. But the impetus for them was inevitably part of the tradition, which reached its greatest political fulfillment in the British common law and the American Declaration of Independence and Constitution. Because of the evil that lies hidden in even the best of human hearts, these values are precious and fragile, hard won by the blood of our ancestors, and in need of constant defense if they are to be preserved. The traditionalist readily admits that the Mosaic Exodus, Socratic inquiry, Roman law, and Christian love were not at all points compatible. Still he thinks that the ways they have interacted in our history have produced a set of ideals, consistent at their core, that give us hope in this world as well as the one to come; that give us, in fact, a foundation for building a better world.

But a certain type of postmodernist thinker looks at this confluence and sees nothing but a pestilent congregation of vapors. Choosing to focus on the tensions rather than the felicities in the complex ways the four strands have interacted, she naturally sees nothing but contradictions. Choosing to focus on the West's failures to live up to its own ideals, she blinds herself to the ways in which they have nevertheless given a liberation to the human spirit which it has found nowhere else. Reading history through the lens of her own jaded cynicism, she can see nothing but power being exercised for its own self-preservation. To her the ideals for which the American Founding Fathers pledged their lives, their fortunes, and their sacred honor are nothing but excuses for the wealthy to hang on to position and power and deny it to everyone else. Christianity is just the white man's religion, reason the white man's way of thinking, lofty ideals just the white man's smokescreen for his real agenda: keeping women and minorities in perpetual subjection.

To the traditionalist, the paradigm of Western civilization as the great oppressor of women and minorities, which exists only by systematically excluding them, is a curious construct indeed. Never mind that this civilization has never permitted—indeed, stands out among human cultures by condemning as barbaric—such "enlightened" customs as foot-binding, female genital mutilation, the veil, or suttee. To try to put our imperfect record on human rights in perspective thus would be to imply that there is some absolute standard by which all societies, including our own, can be measured and that, being a particularly Western idea, must itself be a "tool of the oppressor." When the mind is its own place, perception counts as reality. And many women and members of minority groups do perceive themselves, understandably given the mistreatment to which they have been and can still be subjected, as oppressed.

So how, my postmodernist friends might ask me, are black persons who feel marginalized and excluded by a still WASP-dominated society to consider the heritage of Western civilization as their patrimony? (Alert readers will have noted that not all of the individuals I have listed as bearers of the tradition were white, and many were neither Anglo-Saxon nor Protestant. But we are characterizing the caricature of the tradition as it is often encountered from the postmodernist left in an American context.) Perhaps by considering that there could have been no "Letter from a Birmingham Jail" if there had not first been Thoreau's "Essay on Civil Disobedience." And there could have been no "Essay on Civil Disobedience" unless there had first been Milton's "Areopagetica." And there could have been no "Areopagetica" unless there had first been Plato's "Apology of Socrates." Thus they might come to see certain dead white European males as their potential liberators rather than as merely the engineers of patriarchy and white hegemony. Thus they might come to see Dr. Martin Luther King Jr. as a fruition of the Western tradition, not its negation. And to realize that, if they do value equal protection under the law and at least the chance to be judged by the content of their character as opposed to the color of their skin, it is precisely Western civilization, that horrible WASP (in its American form) phenomenon, that they had better defend, protect, and transmit to the next generation.

Thus the traditionalist rests his case. But the postmodernist is unimpressed. To her, the mere presence of slavery, segregation, Jim Crow, ongoing racism, sexual harassment, and other evils, in the history and in the present of the West, is sufficient to reduce the traditionalist case to the self-serving set of rationalizations she perceives it to be. When she looks at the church, she sees only its complicity in these evils. She shoves detailed analyses of these phenomena at the traditionalist, who simply shrugs his shoulders and says he has never denied them. Flawed human nature produces them everywhere, he reminds her; his point is not that the West is immune to them but that it alone holds out the promise of something better. But to the postmodernist, that promise, like all human words, is empty air.

Thus the two scholars stand and stare at each other across a huge chasm. They each grow increasingly frustrated with the other, for they are constantly tossing facts and arguments at one another to no avail. Their words fall unheeded into the abyss which divides them. They cannot even, like Frost and his neighbor, cooperate to repair the boundary about whose rationale they disagree. For they are looking at the world through two different sets of presuppositional glasses, causing everything they see to look different. If the Enlightenment devotion to objective truth has indeed been exploded, then truth-claims are *truly* [ahem!] nothing more than the most dishonest of power plays. Philosophy and literature are nothing but class warfare conducted by other means, and the postmodernist is just more honest about the situation. But if we think that this alleged explosion has produced more heat and noise than light, then postmodernist analyses tend to be marked by false sophistication, vitiated by a suffocating reductionism, and to be both morally and intellectually perverse. For these scholars are working constantly to undermine the foundations of the civilization that makes their sheltered academic lives possible.

The difficulty in adjudicating between these two camps lies in the fact that any analysis one might offer is already committed to one of the two paradigms at the outset. Fortunately, only one of them makes real analysis possible. If we point out that postmodernists are constantly trying to convince us that their insights are *true* (which, if they actually believed them, is something they ought not to do), or if we notice their dependence on the all-or-nothing fallacy (if an influence is demonstrated, it is immediately taken as proof of a determinism), or if we call attention to their addiction to reductionism, they will understandably respond that these critiques have validity only within the traditionalist paradigm, which is the very thing they are questioning. But that is precisely the point. The logical distinctions which we have always thought intrinsic to the universe, or at least to the human mind, are dismissed by the postmodernist as arbitrary social constructs. Something there is that doesn't love a wall, that wants it down. But can the postmodernist really escape these distinctions, really live without them? That is the question that must be insistently asked.

We must strike deeper. But how? Perhaps in the first place by asking whether even questioning itself—of anything, including tradition—has any meaning in a paradigm from which all answers are rigorously excluded. The traditionalist does not mind being questioned; self-criticism is demanded by his tradition. Before he builds a wall, he wants to know what he is walling in or walling out and to whom he is likely to give offense. He wants to go behind his father's sayings (though, if he is a Christian, he is willing to stop at his Father's). But having done so, he still finds himself helping his neighbor repair the fence, for he knows that one thing is not another, that A is not non-A, that some things are really right and others wrong, and that therefore some boundaries exist necessarily.

More importantly, the postmodernist knows these things too, though she does not want to admit it. She becomes a secret, closet traditionalist every time she pulls up to a stoplight, types an e-mail address into her computer, or orders a pizza. Why? Because reality refuses to cooperate with the theory that there is no right and wrong, or that A is in fact non-A, or that words have no meaning that connects with the world outside the speaker's mind. If a deconstructionist sends back an anchovy pizza on the grounds that she had ordered pepperoni, she destroys her own position; she shows that, whatever she may say when she is theorizing, she actually does expect her words to connect with objective realities in the external world. That's why the traditionalist does not hold with a kind of questioning in which all answers, all legitimate boundaries, are excluded from the outset, all fences by definition arbitrary exercises of power. He sees no point in *that* kind of outdoor game, a game that can only be played on the

protected field of academic theory but which does not apply—*cannot*
be applied—to real life outside the cloistered halls guarded by ivy and
tenure. The traditionalist is right because reality constantly forces the
postmodernist, unintentionally and unwillingly, tacitly but unavoidably, to admit that this is so.

Perhaps a second way of striking deeper is to ask insistently what
it is that we human beings really value. Which is really our gold:
goodness, truth, and beauty (for Christians, as the manifestations
of God's character, his Word, and his glory), or "the endless free
play of the mind in the text"? That, indeed, is the question. Paths
sunder, paradigms are committed to, and interpretive communities
are formed at precisely this point. But note carefully: The postmodernist may simply answer that any value judgment is also a product of the traditionalist view. But she cannot avoid making them
herself. Postmodernists surreptitiously sneak back onto traditionalist
ground again here too. They think that the free play of the mind is
good; they treat it as *true* that there is no truth. They really try to
have it both ways, but they cannot have it both ways. Either truth
exists and can be known, or it does not. Either words have a meaning
that can be discerned in context, or they do not. Good and evil are
either objective realities accessible to the human mind, or they can
be no more than subjective preferences. But no postmodernist can
actually live as if words have no meaning, etc. For these disjunctions
entail one another. Everything follows from that.

With these matters the church must be fundamentally concerned,
especially as it manifests itself in those Protestant traditions that have
always prided themselves on being the church's most consistent and
full-orbed proponents of the truth with which it is entrusted. For
though the church is not identical to Western tradition and indeed
must sometimes stand against it, it has contributed a great deal to
the church and is valuable to her. If the West goes down under this
assault (considered as an attack on the possibility of truth claims),

she will go down with it (insofar as making a particular set of truth claims is the essence of her mission). If the church survives intact, tradition will survive with her, as the best of classical Greece and Rome did when preserved in monastery libraries in the Middle Ages. If the church survives by acquiescing in the destruction of the Western tradition, she will be transformed into something that can no longer be called "the household of God, which is the Church of the living God, the pillar and support of the truth" (1 Tim. 3:15 NASB).

God of course will not allow that ultimate acquiescence and transformation to happen, for he always preserves a faithful remnant; but nevertheless, much damage will be done if we are not vigilant. It has already been done, in our failure sufficiently to arm our young people and prepare them to defend themselves against this new threat, and in our slowness to realize the need to supplement our old apologetic, directed against a modernist foe which has long been passé. Yet there is reason for hope that such vigilance may be fruitful even without appealing to remnant theology. If there is no objective difference between gold and iron pyrite, people are not going to commit themselves to serious prospecting. And I have a sneaking suspicion that with no foul lines, no bases, and no way to keep score, this free play of the mind is a game that will quickly produce an *ennui* more intense and a disillusionment more deep than any we have seen since the collapse of Rome. Boredom and barbarism may then seem to be the only options available. We may in fact be entering such a time already. It is surely part of our calling to keep some memory of both Western civilization and Christian truth alive and vibrant enough to serve as a viable alternative to those terrible choices in that day.

Postlude

THE QUEST MOTIF

(What C. S. Lewis and J. R. R. Tolkien Knew, And Peter Jackson Does Not)
Sonnet CI

Snaking out across the vast expanse
  Of history and legend lies a trail,
  The footing treacherous, the markings pale,
And peril lies in wait for those who chance
To travel it. But if they can advance,
  And if their luck and courage do not fail,
  They may emerge into a mystic vale
And reach the magic realm of fair romance.

The landscape's always changing. There is no
  Map that can be trusted once you swerve
  Aside; your only compass is your quest.
If, true to friend, implacable to foe,
  You're faithful to the vision that you serve,
  You'll find that country which the muse has blessed.

—D.T.W.

LIST OF WORKS
CONSULTED

"My library / Was dukedom large enough."

—PROSPERO, IN SHAKESPEARE'S *THE TEMPEST*

Abromaitis, C. N. Sue. "The Distant Mirror of Middle Earth: The Sacramental Vision of J. R. R. Tolkien." *Touchstone* 15:1 (January–February 2002): 33–39.

Adey, Lionel. *C. S. Lewis: Writer, Dreamer, and Mentor.* Grand Rapids: Eerdmans, 1998.

Adler, Mortimer J. *Ten Philosophical Mistakes.* New York: Macmillan, 1985.

Aeschliman, Michael D. *The Restitution of Man: C. S. Lewis and the Case against Scientism.* Grand Rapids: Eerdmans, 1983, rpt. 1998.

Barfield, Owen. *Owen Barfield on C. S. Lewis.,* ed. G. B. Tennyson. Middletown, Conn.: Wesleyan University Press, 1989.

Bauman, Michael. *Pilgrim Theology: Taking the Path of Theological Discovery.* Grand Rapids: Zondervan, 1992.

Berkhof, Louis. *Systematic Theology.* 4th revised and enlarged ed. Grand Rapids: Eerdmans, 1939.

Berkouwer, G. C. *Man: The Image of God.* Studies in Dogmatics, vol. 8. Grand Rapids: Eerdmans, 1962.

Beversluis, John. *C. S. Lewis and the Search for Rational Religion.* Grand Rapids: Eerdmans, 1985.

Blamires, Harry. "Teaching the Universal Truth: C. S. Lewis among the Intellectuals." In David Mills, ed., *The Pilgrim's Guide: C. S. Lewis and the Art of Witness.* Grand Rapids: Eerdmans, 1998: 15–26.

——————. *The Christian Mind.* London: S.P.C.K., 1963.

Brewer, Derek S. "*The Lord of the Rings* as Romance." In *J. R. R. Tolkien, Scholar and Storyteller: Essays* in Memoriam, ed. Mary Salu and Robert T. Farrell. Ithaca: Cornell University Press, 1979: 249–64.

Brown, Colin. *Philosophy and the Christian Faith: An Introduction to the Main Thinkers and Schools of Thought from the Middle Ages to the Present Day.* Downers Grove, Ill.: InterVarsity Press, 1968.

Brown, Devin. *Inside Narnia: A Guide to Exploring The Lion, the Witch and the Wardrobe.* Grand Rapids: Baker, 2005.

Brown, Harold O. J. *The Sensate Culture: Western Civilization between Chaos and Transformation.* Dallas: Word, 1996.

Burson, Scott R. and Jerry L. Walls. *C. S. Lewis and Francis Schaeffer: Lessons for a New Century from the Most Influential Apologists of Our Time.* Downers Grove, Ill.: IVP, 1998.

Burt, Donald X., O.S.A. *Friendship and Society: An Introduction to Augustine's Practical Philosophy.* Grand Rapids: Eerdmans, 1999.

Caldecott, Stratford. "The Lord and Lady of the Rings: The Hidden Presence of Tolkien's Catholicism in *The Lord of the Rings.*" *Touchstone* 15:1 (January–February 2002): 51–57.

Calvin, John. *Institutes of the Christian Religion.* Trans. Henry Beveridge. 2 vols. Grand Rapids: Eerdmans, 1975.

Carnell, Corbin Scott. *Bright Shadow of Reality: C. S. Lewis and the Feeling Intellect.* Grand Rapids: Eerdmans, 1974.

Carpenter, Humphrey. *The Inklings.* Boston: Houghton Mifflin, 1979.

——————. *Tolkien: The Authorized Biography.* Boston: Houghton Mifflin, 1977.

Carter, Lin. *Tolkien: A Look behind "The Lord of the Rings."* New York: Ballantine, 1969.

Cary, George. *I Believe in Man.* Grand Rapids: Eerdmans, 1977.

Cary, Norman Reed. *Christian Criticism in the Twentieth Century.* Port Washington, New York: Kennicat Press., 1975.

Chesterton, G. K. *The Everlasting Man.* New York: Dodd, Mead, and Company, 1925.

—————. *Orthodoxy.* Garden City, New York: Doubleday, 1959.

Christopher, Joe R. *C. S. Lewis.* Twayne's English Authors Series. Boston: G. K. Hall, 1987.

Clark, Gordon H. *A Christian View of Men and Things.* Grand Rapids: Eerdmans, 1952.

—————. "Image of God." *Baker's Dictionary of Christian Ethics,* ed. Carl F. H. Henry. Grand Rapids: Baker, 1973: 312–13.

Como, James. *Branches to Heaven: The Geniuses of C. S. Lewis.* Dallas: Spence Publishing Co., 1998.

Conlon, D. J., ed. *G. K. Chesterton: A Half Century of Views.* Oxford: Oxford University Press, 1987.

Coren, Michael. *Gilbert: The Man Who Was G. K. Chesterton.* New York: Paragon House, 1990.

Crabbe, Katharyn W. *J. R. R. Tolkien.* New York: Continuum, 1988.

Cunningham, Richard B. *C. S. Lewis: Defender of the Faith.* Philadelphia: Westminster Press, 1967.

Dale, Alzina Stone. *The Outline of Sanity: A Life of G. K. Chesterton.* Grand Rapids: Eerdmans, 1981.

Dickerson, Matthew. *Following Gandalf: Epic Battles and Moral Victory in The Lord of the Rings.* Grand Rapids: Brazos, 2003.

Dockery, David S., ed. *The Challenge of PostModernism: An Evangelical Engagement.* Wheaton: Bridgepoint, 1995.

Dowie, William. "The Gospel of Middle Earth according to J. R. R. Tolkien." In Mary Salu and Robert T. Farrell, eds. *J. R. R. Tolkien, Scholar and Storyteller: Essays* in Memoriam. Ithaca: Cornell University Press, 1979: 265–85.

Downing, David C. *Into the Region of Awe: Mysticism in C. S. Lewis.*
Downers Grove, Ill.: InterVarsity Press, 2005.

————. *The Most Reluctant Convert: C. S. Lewis's Journey to Faith.*
Downers Grove, Ill.: InterVarsity Press, 2002.

————. *Planets in Peril: A Critical Study of C. S. Lewis's Ransom
Trilogy.* Amherst: University of Massachusetts Press, 1992.

D'Souza, Dinesh. "Multiculturalism: Fact or Threat?" *Imprimis* 30:9
(September 2001): 1–5.

Dunlap, Ruby. "Common Minds: A Study of Metaphors of Good and Evil
across Language Groups." Diss. Tennessee State University, 2002.

Duriez, Colin. *The J. R. R. Tolkien Handbook: A Comprehensive Guide
to His Life, Writings, and World of Middle Earth.* Grand Rapids:
Baker, 1992.

Edwards, Bruce. *Further Up and Further In: Understanding C. S. Lewis's
The Lion, the Witch and the Wardrobe.* Nashville: Broadman &
Holman, 2005.

Edwards, Bruce L., Jr., *A Rhetoric of Reading: C. S. Lewis's Defense of
Western Literacy.* Provo, Utah: Center for the Study of Christian
Values in Literature, College of Humanities, Brigham Young
University, 1986.

————, ed. *The Taste of the Pineapple: Essays on C. S. Lewis as
Reader, Critic, and Imaginative Writer.* Bowling Green, Ohio:
Bowling Green State University Press, 1988.

————. "A Thoroughly Converted Man: C. S. Lewis in the Public
Square." In David Mills, ed., *The Pilgrim's Guide: C. S. Lewis and
the Art of Witness.* Grand Rapids: Eerdmans, 1998: 27–39.

Eliot, T. S. "The Social Function of Poetry." 1943; rpt. *On Poetry and
Poets.* New York: Noonday Press, 1961: 3–16.

————. "Tradition and the Individual Talent." *Selected Essays,* new
ed. New York: Harcourt, Brace, & Co., 1950: 3–11.

Ellis, John M. *Literature Lost: Social Agendas and the Corruption of the
Humanities.* New Haven: Yale University Press, 1997.

Ellwood, Gracia Fay. *Good News from Tolkien's Middle Earth.* Grand
Rapids: Eerdmans, 1970.

Evans, Maurice. *G. K. Chesterton: The Le Bas Prize Essay.* Cambridge:
Cambridge University Press, 1938; rpt. New York: Haskell House,
1972.

Fagerberg, David W. "Splendor in the Ordinary: On Chesterton's
Incarnational Style." *Touchstone* 14:7 (September 2001): 18–20.

Filmer, Kath. *The Fiction of C. S. Lewis: Mask and Mirror.* New York:
St. Martin's Press, 1993.

Flieger, Verlyn. "Fantasy and Reality: J. R. R. Tolkien's World and the
Fairy Story Essay." *Mythlore* 22:3 (Winter 1999): 4–13.

————. *Splintered Light: Logos and Language in Tolkien's World.*
Grand Rapids: Eerdmans, 1983.

————. "A Question of Time." *Mythlore* 16:3 (Spring 1990): 5–8.

Foster, Robert. *A Guide to Middle Earth: A Complete and Definitive
Concordance for "The Lord of the Rings."* New York: Ballantine,
1971.

Gardner, John. *Grendel.* New York: Vintage Books, 1989.

————. *On Moral Fiction.* New York: Basic Books, 1978.

Gibb, Jocelyn, ed. *Light on C. S. Lewis.* New York: Harcourt, Brace, &
World, 1965.

Gilbert, Douglas and C. S. Kilby. *C. S. Lewis: Images of his World.* Grand
Rapids: Eerdmans, 1973.

Glaspey, Terry W. *Not a Tame Lion: The Spiritual Legacy of C. S. Lewis.*
Nashville: Cumberland House, 1996.

Glover, Donald E. *C. S. Lewis: The Art of Enchantment.* Athens, Ohio:
Ohio University Press, 1985.

Goffar, Janine. *The C. S. Lewis Index: A Comprehensive Guide to Lewis's
Writings and Ideas.* Wheaton: Crossway, 1995.

Graff, Gerald. *Literature against Itself: Literary Ideas in Modern Society.*
With a new preface by the author. Chicago: Dee, 1995.

Green, Roger Lancelyn and Walter Hooper. *C. S. Lewis: A Biography.*
New York: Harcourt Brace Jovanovich, 1974.

Greene, Deirdre. "Higher Argument: Tolkien and the Tradition of Vision, Epic, and Prophecy." *Mythlore* 21:2 (Winter 1996): 45–52.

Gregersen, Niels Henrik, Wellem B. Drees, and Ulf Gorman, eds., *The Human Person in Science and Technology*. Grand Rapids: Eerdmans, 2000.

Gresham, Douglas H. *Lenten Lands: My Childhood with Joy Davidman and C. S. Lewis*. New York: Macmillan, 1988.

Groothuis, Douglas. *Truth Decay: Defending Christianity against the Challenges of Postmodernism*. Downers Grove, Ill.: InterVarsity Press, 2000.

Hart, Dabney Adams. *Through the Open Door: A New Look at C. S. Lewis*. University, Ala.: University of Alabama Press, 1984.

Heim, Karl. *Christian Faith and Natural Science*. San Francisco: Harper & Row, 1953; rpt. Gloucester, Mass.: Peter Smith, 1971.

Helms, Randel. *Tolkien and the Silmarils*. Boston: Houghton Mifflin, 1981.

—————. *Tolkien's World*. Boston: Houghton Mifflin, 1974.

Hollis, Christopher. *The Mind of Chesterton*. Coral Gables, Fla.: University of Miami Press, 1970.

Hood, Gwyneth. "The Earthly Paradise in Tolkien's *The Lord of the Rings*." *Mythlore* 21:2 (Winter 1996): 139–44.

Hooper, Walter. *Past Watchful Dragons: The Narnian Chronicles of C. S. Lewis*. New York: Harper Collins, 1971, rpt. 1979.

Hughes, Philip Edgcumbe. *The True Image: The Origin and Destiny of Man in Christ*. Grand Rapids: Eerdmans, 1989; rpt. Eugene, Ore.: Wipf & Stock, 2001.

Huttar, Charles, ed. *Imagination and the Spirit: Essays in Literature and the Christian Faith Presented to Clyde S. Kilby*. Grand Rapids: Eerdmans, 1971.

—————. "A Lifelong Love Affair with Language: C. S. Lewis's Poetry." In *Word and Story in C. S. Lewis*. Ed. Peter J. Schakel and Charles A. Huttar. Columbia: University of Missouri Press, 1991: 86–108.

Huxley, Aldous. *Brave New World*. New York: Harper & Row, 1946.

Isaacs, Neil D. and Rose A. Zimbardo, eds. *Tolkien and the Critics: Essays on J. R. R. Tolkien and "The Lord of the Rings."* Notre Dame: University of Notre Dame Press, 1968.

——————, eds. *Tolkien: New Critical Perspectives.* Lexington: University of Kentucky Press, 1981.

Jeffrey, David Lyle. *People of the Book: Christian Identity and Literary Culture.* Grand Rapids: Eerdmans, 1996.

Kantzer, Kenneth Sealer. "John Calvin's Theory of the Knowledge of God and the Word of God." Diss. Harvard, 1950.

——————. "Man, Doctrine of." *Baker's Dictionary of Christian Ethics.* Ed. Carl F. H. Henry. Grand Rapids: Baker, 1973: 403–6.

Keefe, Carolyn, ed. *C. S. Lewis: Speaker and Teacher.* Grand Rapids: Zondervan, 1971.

Kilby, Clyde S. *The Christian World of C. S. Lewis.* Grand Rapids: Eerdmans, 1964.

——————. *Christianity and Aesthetics.* Chicago: InterVarsity Press, 1961.

——————. *Images of Salvation in the Fiction of C. S. Lewis.* Wheaton: Harold Shaw, 1978.

——————. *Tolkien and "The Silmarillion."* Wheaton: Harold Shaw, 1976.

Kimball, Roger. *Tenured Radicals: How Politics Has Corrupted Higher Education.* Rev. ed., with a new Introduction by the author. Chicago: Dee, 1998.

Kocher, Paul H. *Master of Middle Earth: The Fiction of J. R. R. Tolkien.* Boston: Houghton Mifflin, 1972.

Kort, Wesley A. *C. S. Lewis, Then and Now.* Oxford: Oxford University Press, 2001.

Kreeft, Peter. *Back to Virtue: Traditional Moral Wisdom for Modern Moral Confusion.* San Francisco: Ignatius, 1992.

——————. *C. S. Lewis for the Third Millennium: Six Essays on "The Abolition of Man."* San Francisco: Ignatius Press, 1994.

Lakoff, George. *Women, Fire, and Dangerous Things: What Categories Reveal about the Mind.* Chicago: University of Chicago Press, 1987.

Lakoff, George and Mark Johnson. *Metaphors We Live By.* Chicago: University of Chicago Press, 1980.

Lawlor, John. *C. S. Lewis: Memories and Reflections.* Dallas: Spence Pub. Co., 1998.

Lewis, C. S. *The Abolition of Man.* Ontario: Macmillan, 1947.

—————. "Bluspels and Flalansferes: A Semantic Nightmare." In *Selected Literary Essays,* ed. Walter Hooper. Cambridge: Cambridge University Press, 1969: 251–65.

—————. "Christianity and Culture." *Theology* 40 (March 1940): 166–79; rpt. *Christian Reflections.* Ed. Walter Hooper. Grand Rapids: Eerdmans, 1967: 12–36.

—————. "Christianity and Literature." *Rehabilitations and Other Essays.* Oxford, 1939. rpt. *Christian Reflections,* 1–11.

—————. "A Confession." Orig. pub. as "Spartan Nactus." *Punch* 227 (1 December 1954): 685; rpt. *Poems.* Ed. Walter Hooper. New York: Harcourt Brace Jovanovich, 1964: 1.

—————. "De Descriptione Temporum." 1955; rpt. *Selected Literary Essays.* Ed. Walter Hooper. Cambridge: Cambridge University Press, 1969: 1–14.

—————. *The Discarded Image: An Introduction to Medieval and Renaissance Literature.* Cambridge: Cambridge University Press, 1964.

—————. "Eden's Courtesy." In *Poems.* Ed. Walter Hooper. New York: Harcourt Brace Jovanovich, 1964: 98.

—————. *English Literature in the Sixteenth Century, Excluding Drama. The Oxford History of English Literature.* Oxford: The Oxford University Press, 1954.

—————. *An Experiment in Criticism.* Cambridge: Cambridge University Press, 1961.

————. "An Expostulation against Too Many Writers of Science Fiction." *Magazine of Fantasy and Science Fiction* 16 (June 1959): 47; rpt. *Poems,* 58.

————. *The Four Loves.* New York: Harcourt, Brace & World, 1960.

————. *The Horse and His Boy.* New York: HarperCollins, 1978.

————. "The Inner Ring." 1944. Rpt. *The Weight of Glory and Other Addresses.* Grand Rapids: Eerdmans, 1965: 55–66.

————. "The Language of Religion." Address from ca. 1953, first pub. in *Christian Reflections,* 129–41.

————. *The Last Battle.* New York: HarperCollins, 1978.

————. "Lilies that Fester." *The Twentieth Century,* April 1955; rpt. in *The World's Last Night and Other Essays.* New York: Harcourt Brace & World, 1960: 31–49.

————. *The Lion, the Witch and the Wardrobe.* New York: HarperCollins, 1978.

————. *The Magician's Nephew.* New York: HarperCollins, 1978.

————. "Man Is a Lumpe Where All Beasts Kneaded Be." *Oxford Magazine* 52 (10 May 1934): 665; rpt. *Poems,* 68.

————. "Meditation in a Toolshed." *God in the Dock,* ed. Walter Hooper. Grand Rapids: Eerdmans, 1970: 212–15.

————. *Mere Christianity.* New York: Macmillan, 1943.

————. *Miracles: A Preliminary Study.* New York: Macmillan, 1947.

————. "On the Reading of Old Books." Preface to St. Athanasius, *The Incarnation of the Word of God,* trans. A Religious of C.S.M.V. Bles, 1944; rpt. *God in the Dock,* ed. Walter Hooper. Grand Rapids: Eerdmans, 1970: 200–7.

————. "On Three Ways of Writing for Children." The Library Association. *Proceedings, Papers, and Summaries of Discussions at the Bournemouth Conference, 29 April to 2 May 1952*; rpt. *Of Other Worlds,* ed. Walter Hooper. New York: Harcourt, Brace, Jovanovich, 1964: 22–34.

————. *Out of the Silent Planet.* 1938. Reprint, New York: Simon & Schuster Inc., 1996.

———. *Perelandra*. 1943. Reprint New York: Simon & Schuster Inc., 1996.

———. *The Pilgrim's Regress: An Apology for Christianity Reason and Romanticism*. 1933; rpt. Grand Rapids: Eerdmans, 1958.

———. "The Poison of Subjectivism." *Religion and Life* 12 (1943); rpt. *Christian Reflections*, ed. Walter Hooper. Grand Rapids: Eerdmans, 1967.

———. *A Preface to Paradise Lost*. London: Oxford University Press, 1962.

———. *Prince Caspian*. New York: HarperCollins, 1978.

———. *The Problem of Pain*. New York: Macmillan, 1967.

———. *The Screwtape Letters and Screwtape Proposes a Toast*. With a new preface by the author. New York: Macmillan, 1961.

———. *The Silver Chair*. New York: HarperCollins, 1978.

———. "Sometimes Fairy Stories May Say Best What's to Be Said." *New York Times Book Review, Children's Book Section*, November 1956; rpt. *Of Other Worlds*, op. cit.: 35–38.

———. *Surprised by Joy: The Shape of My Early Life*. New York: Harcourt, Brace, & World, 1955.

———. *That Hideous Strength* 1945. Reprint, New York: Simon & Schuster, 1996.

———. *'Till We Have Faces: A Myth Retold*. Harcourt Brace & World, 1956; rpt. Grand Rapids: Eerdmans, 1968.

———. *The Voyage of the Dawn Treader*. New York: HarperCollins, 1978.

———. *The Weight of Glory*. New York: Macmillan, 1949. Published in England under the title *Transposition and Other Addresses*.

Lewis, Gordon. In "An Integrative Method of Justifying Religious Assertions." *Evangelical Apologetics: Selected Essays from the 1995 Evangelical Theological Society Convention*. Ed. Michael Bauman, David Hall, and Robert Newman. Camp Hill, Penn.: Christian Publications, 1996: 69–88.

Lewis, Warren H. *Brothers and Friends: The Diaries of Major Warren Hamilton Lewis.* Ed. Clyde S. Kilby and Marjorie Lamp Mead. New York: Ballantine, 1982.

Lindskoog, Kathryn. *Finding the Landlord: A Guidebook to C. S. Lewis's "Pilgrim's Regress."* Chicago: Cornerstone Press, 1995.

——————. *Light in the Shadowlands: Protecting the Real C. S. Lewis.* Sisters, Ore.: Multnomah, 1994.

——————. *The Lion of Judah in Never-Never Land.* Grand Rapids: Eerdmans, 1973.

——————. *Surprised by C. S. Lewis, George MacDonald, and Dante: An Array of Original Discoveries.* Macon: Mercer University Press, 2001.

——————. *The C. S. Lewis Hoax.* Portland: Multnomah, 1988.

Lucas, J. R. "Restoration of Man: A Lecture Given in Durham on Thursday October 22, 1992 by J. R. Lucas to Mark the Fiftieth Anniversary of C. S. Lewis's '*The Abolition of Man.*'" 7 March 2003. http://users.ox.ac.uk/~jrlucas/lewis.html.

MacDonald, Michael H. and Andrew Tadie, eds. *The Riddle of Joy: G. K. Chesterton and C. S. Lewis.* Grand Rapids: Eerdmans, 1989.

Manlove, Colin N. *C. S. Lewis: His Literary Achievement.* New York: St. Martin's Press, 1987.

——————. *The Chronicles of Narnia: The Patterning of a Fantastic World.* New York: Twayne Publishers, 1993.

Markos, Louis. *Lewis Agonistes: How C. S. Lewis Can Train Us to Wrestle with the Modern and Postmodern World.* Nashville: Broadman & Holman, 2003.

Martin, Thomas L., ed. *Reading the Classics with C. S. Lewis.* Grand Rapids: Baker, 2000.

Meilaender, Gilbert. *The Taste for the Other: The Social and Ethical Thought of C. S. Lewis.* Grand Rapids: Eerdmans, 1978.

Menuge, Angus J. L., ed. *C. S. Lewis, Lightbearer in the Shadowlands: The Evangelistic Vision of C. S. Lewis.* Wheaton: Crossway, 1997.

Mills, David, ed. *The Pilgrim's Guide: C. S. Lewis and the Art of Witness.* Grand Rapids: Eerdmans, 1998.

—————. Review of *Tolkien: A Celebration.* Ed. Joseph Pearce (San Francisco: Ignatius, 2001), in *Touchstone* 15:1 (January–February 2002): 59–63.

—————. "The Writer of Our Story: Divine Providence in 'The Lord of the Rings.'" *Touchstone* 15:1 (January–February 2002): 22–28.

Milton, John. *Complete Poems and Major Prose.* Ed. Merritt Y. Hughes. Indianapolis: Bobbs-Merrill, 1957.

Mitchell, Christopher W. "Bearing the Weight of Glory: The Cost of C. S. Lewis's Witness." In David Mills, ed., *The Pilgrim's Guide: C. S. Lewis and the Art of Witness.* Grand Rapids: Eerdmans, 1998: 3–14.

Montaigne, Michel de. *Montaigne's Essays and Selected Writings: A Bilingual Edition.* Trans. Donald M. Frame. New York: St. Martin's Press, 1963.

Montgomery, John Warwick, ed. *Myth, Allegory, and Gospel: An Interpretation of J. R. R. Tolkien, C. S. Lewis, G. K. Chesterton, and Charles Williams.* Minneapolis: Bethany, 1974.

Montgomery, Marion. *The Truth of Things: Liberal Arts and the Recovery of Reality.* Dallas: Spence Publishing Co., 1999.

Moreland, J. P. "Philosophical Apologetics, the Church, and Contemporary Culture." In *Evangelical Apologetics: Selected Essays from the 1995 Evangelical Theological Society Convention,* ed. Michael Bauman, David Hall, and Robert Newman. Camp Hill, Pa.: Christian Publications, 1996: 3–33.

Nash, Ronald H. *Life's Ultimate Questions: An Introduction to Philosophy.* Grand Rapids: Zondervan, 1999.

Nelson, Dale. "Rings of Love: J. R. R. Tolkien and the Four Loves." *Touchstone* 15:1 (January–February 2002): 48–50.

—————. "Tolkien and the Perennial Tradition." *Mallorn: The Journal of the Tolkien Society* 39 (September 2000): 39–40.

Newman, Robert C. "Scientific Problems for Scientism." In *Evangelical Apologetics: Selected Essays from the 1995 Evangelical Theological Society Convention,* ed. Michael Bauman, David Hall, and Robert Newman. Camp Hill, Pa.: Christian Publications, 1996: 245–68.

Nicholi, Armand M., Jr. *The Question of God: C. S. Lewis and Sigmund Freud Debate God, Love, Sex, and the Meaning of Life.* New York: Free Press, 2002.

Noyes, Russell, ed. *English Romantic Poetry and Prose.* New York: Oxford University Press, 1956.

Oden, Thomas C. "Christian Apologetics in a Non-Christian World." *Evangelical Apologetics: Selected Essays from the 1995 Evangelical Theological Society Convention,* ed. Michael Bauman, David Hall, and Robert Newman. Camp Hill, Penn.: Christian Publications, 1996: 271–93.

Orwell, George. *1984.* With an afterword by Erich Fromm. New York: Harcourt Brace Jovanovich, 1949.

Packer, J. I. "Living Truth for a Dying World: The Message of C. S. Lewis." *Crux* 34:4 (December 1998): 3–12; reprint *The J. I. Packer Collection.* ed. Alister McGrath. Downers Grove, Ill.: InterVarsity Press, 1999: 269–84.

—————. "On from Orr: The Cultural Crisis, Rational Realism, and Incarnational Ontology." *Crux* 32:3 (September 1996): 12–26. rpt. *The J. I. Packer Collection.* ed. Alister McGrath. Downers Grove, Ill.: InterVarsity Press, 1999: 244–68.

Parker, Douglass. "Hwaet We Holbytla." *Hudson Review* 9:4 (Winter 1956–57): 598–609.

Patrick, James. "The Heart's Desire and the Landlord's Rules: C. S. Lewis as Moral Philosopher." In David Mills, ed., *The Pilgrim's Guide: C. S. Lewis and the Art of Witness.* Grand Rapids: Eerdmans, 1998: 70–85.

—————. *The Magdalen Metaphysicals: Idealism and Orthodoxy at Oxford, 1901–1945.* Macon, Ga.: Mercer University Press, 1985.

Pearce, Joseph, ed. *Tolkien: A Celebration.* San Francisco: Ignatius, 2001.

──────. *Tolkien: Man and Myth.* San Francisco: Ignatius, 1998.

Penrose, Roger. *The Emperor's New Mind: Concerning Computers, Minds, and the Laws of Physics.* New York: Penguin, 1991.

Peters, Thomas C. *Battling for the Modern Mind: A Beginner's Chesterton.* St. Louis: Concordia, 1994.

──────. *The Christian Imagination: G. K. Chesterton on the Arts.* San Francisco: Ignatius, 2000.

Piper, John and Wayne Grudem, eds. *Recovering Biblical Manhood and Womanhood: A Response to Evangelical Feminism.* Wheaton: Crossway, 1991.

Podles, Leon J. "The Heroes of Middle Earth: J. R. R. Tolkien and the Marks of Christian Heroism." *Touchstone* 15:1 (January–February 2002): 29–32.

Polanyi, Michael. *Personal Knowledge: Towards a Post-Critical Philosophy.* New York: Harper & Row, 1964.

──────. *The Study of Man.* Chicago: University of Chicago Press, 1959.

Pope, Alexander. "An Essay on Man." *The Poems of Alexander Pope,* ed. John Butt. New Haven: Yale University Press, 1963: 501–47.

Pratchett, Terry. *Thief of Time.* New York: HarperCollins, 2001.

Purtill, Richard. *Lord of Elves and Eldils: Fantasy and Philosophy in C. S. Lewis and J. R. R. Tolkien.* Grand Rapids: Zondervan, 1974.

Pyne, Robert H. *Humanity and Sin: The Creation, Fall, and Redemption of Humanity.* Nashville: Word, 1999.

Rapp, Carl. *Fleeing the Universal: The Critique of Post-Rational Criticism.* Albany: State University of New York Press, 1998.

Reppert, Victor. *C. S. Lewis's Dangerous Idea: In Defense of the Argument from Reason.* Downers Grove, Ill.: InterVarsity Press, 2003.

──────. "Interview: Dr. Victor Reppert on 'The Argument from Reason.'" Quality Christian Internet. 5 March 2003. http://go.qci.tripod.com/Reppert-interview.htm.

—————. "The Lewis-Anscombe Controversy: A Discussion of the Issues." *Christian Scholar's Review* 19:1 (September 1989): 32–48.

Reynolds, Patricia and Glen H. Goodknight, eds., *Proceedings of the J. R. R. Tolkien Centenary Conference, Keble College, Oxford, 1992.* Altadena, Calif.: Mythopoeic Press, 1995.

Ritchie, Daniel E. *Reconstructing Literature in an Ideological Age: A Biblical Poetics and Literary Studies from Milton to Burke.* Grand Rapids: Eerdmans, 1996.

Robinson, H. Wheeler. *The Christian Doctrine of Man.* 2nd ed. Edinburgh: T. & T. Clark, 1913.

Roby, Kinley E. *J. R. R. Tolkien.* Twayne's English Authors Series. Boston: G. K. Hall, 1980.

Ruud, Jay. "Aslan's Sacrifice and the Doctrine of Atonement in *The Lion, the Witch, and the Wardrobe.*" *Mythlore* 23:2 (Spring 2001): 15–22.

Ryken, Leland, ed. *The Christian Imagination: The Practice of Faith in Literature and Writing.* Colorado Springs: Shaw, 2002.

Ryken, Leland, and Marjorie Lamp Mead. *A Reader's Guide through the Wardrobe: Exploring C. S. Lewis's Classic Story.* Downers Grove, Ill.: InterVarsity Press, 2005.

Salu, Mary and Robert T. Farrell, eds. *J. R. R. Tolkien, Scholar and Storyteller: Essays* in Memoriam. Ithaca: Cornell University Press, 1979.

Sayer, George. *Jack: A Life of C. S. Lewis.* Wheaton: Crossway, 1994.

Sayers, Dorothy L. *The Mind of the Maker.* 1941. Rpt. San Francisco: Harper & Row, 1979.

Schaeffer, Francis A. *Art and the Bible.* Downers Grove, Ill.: InterVarsity Press, 1973.

—————. *Back to Freedom and Dignity.* Downers Grove, Ill.: InterVarsity Press, 1972.

—————. *Death in the City.* Downers Grove, Ill.: InterVarsity Press, 1969.

————. *Escape from Reason*. Downers Grove, Ill.: InterVarsity Press, 1968.

————. *Genesis in Space and Time: The Flow of Biblical History*. Downers Grove, Ill.: InterVarsity Press, 1972.

————. *The God Who Is There: Speaking Historic Christianity into the Twentieth Century*. Downers Grove, Ill.: InterVarsity Press, 1968.

————. *He Is There and He Is Not Silent*. Wheaton, Ill.: Tyndale House, 1972.

————. *Pollution and the Death of Man: The Christian View of Ecology*. Wheaton, Ill.: Tyndale House, 1970.

Schakel, Peter J. "The 'Correct' Order for Reading the Chronicles of Narnia." *Mythlore* 23:2 (Spring 2001): 4–14.

————. *Imagination and the Arts in C. S. Lewis: Journeying to Narnia and Other Worlds*. Columbia: University of Missouri Press, 2002.

————., ed. *The Longing for a Form: Essays on the Fiction of C. S. Lewis*. Grand Rapids: Baker, 1977.

————. *Reading with the Heart: The Way into Narnia*. Grand Rapids: Eerdmans, 1979.

————. *Reason and Imagination in C. S. Lewis: A Study of 'Till We Have Faces*. Grand Rapids: Eerdmans, 1984.

Schultz, Jefferey D. and John G. West Jr., eds. *The C. S. Lewis Reader's Encyclopedia*. Grand Rapids: Zondervan, 1998.

Schweicher, Eric. "Aspects of the Fall in *The Silmarillion*." *Mythlore* 21:2 (Winter 1996): 167–71.

Scull, Christina. "Open Minds, Closed Minds in *The Lord of the Rings*." *Mythlore* 21:2 (Winter 1996): 151–56.

Shakespeare, William. *Shakespeare: The Complete Works*, ed. G. B. Harrison. New York: Harcourt, Brace & World, 1968.

Shaw, Luci. "C. S. Lewis: The Light in the Kilns." *Christianity and Literature* 52:1 (Autumn 2002): 34.

Shippey, T. A. "Creation from Philology in *The Lord of the Rings*." In *J. R. R. Tolkien, Scholar and Storyteller: Essays* in Memoriam. Mary

Salu and Robert T. Farrell, eds. Ithaca: Cornell University Press, 1979: 286–316.

————. *J. R. R. Tolkien: Author of the Century.* Boston: Houghton Mifflin, 2000.

————. *The Road to Middle Earth.* London: Allen & Unwin, 1982.

Shippey, Tom. "Tolkien and the Gawain Poet." *Mythlore* 21:2 (Winter 1996): 213–19.

Sims, John A. *Missionaries to the Skeptics: Christian Apologists for the Twentieth Century—C. S. Lewis, Edward John Carnell, and Reinhold Niebuhr.* Macon, Ga.: Mercer University Press, 1995.

Skinner, B. F. *Beyond Freedom and Dignity.* New York: Bantam, 1971.

Smith, Mark Eddy. *Tolkien's Ordinary Virtues: Exploring the Spiritual Themes of* "The Lord of the Rings." Downers Grove, Ill.: InterVarsity Press, 2002.

Smith, Roger Houston. *Patches of Godlight: The Pattern of Thought of C. S. Lewis.* Athens: University of Georgia Press, 1981.

Spenser, Edmund. *The Faerie Queene.* 1590. 2 vols. ed. J. C. Smith. Oxford: Oxford University Press, 1909.

Stock, R. D. "The Tao and the Objective Room: A Pattern in C. S. Lewis's Novels." *Christian Scholar's Review* 9:3 (1980): 256–66.

Tetreault, James. "Parallel Lives: C. S. Lewis and T. S. Eliot." *Renascence: Essays on Value in Literature* 38:4 (Summer 1986): 256–59.

Thornhill, John. *Modernity: Christianity's Estranged Child Reconstructed.* Grand Rapids: Eerdmans, 2000.

Thorpe, Dwayne. "Tolkien's Elvish Craft." *Mythlore* 21:2 (Winter 1996): 315–21.

Thorson, Stephen. "Barfield's Evolution of Consciousness: How Much Did Lewis Accept?" *SEVEN: An Anglo-American Literary Review* 15 (1998): 9–35.

————. "'Knowledge' in C. S. Lewis's Post-Conversion Thought: His Epistemological Method." *SEVEN: An Anglo-American Literary Review* 9 (1988): 91–116.

——————. "Lewis and Barfield on Imagination." *Mythlore* 17:2 (Winter 1990): 12–18.

——————. "Lewis and Barfield on Imagination, Part II." *Mythlore* 17:3 (Spring 1991): 16–21.

Tolkien, J. R. R. "Beowulf: The Monsters and the Critics." *Proceedings of the British Academy* 22 (1936): 245–95; reprint *An Anthology of Beowulf Criticism.* Ed. Lewis E. Nicholson. Notre Dame, Indiana: University of Notre Dame Press, 1963: 51–103.

——————. *The Fellowship of the Ring.* New York: Ballantine Books, 1982.

——————. *The Hobbit.* New York: Ballantine Books, 1982.

——————. *The Letters of J. R. R. Tolkien.* Selected and edited by Humphrey Carpenter, with the assistance of Christopher Tolkien. Boston: Houghton Mifflin, 1981.

——————. "On Faerie Stories." In *The Tolkien Reader.* New York: Ballantine, 1966: 3–84.

——————. *The Return of the King.* New York: Ballantine Books, 1982.

——————. *The Silmarillion.* Boston: Houghton Mifflin Co., 1977.

——————. *The Two Towers.* New York: Ballantine Books, 1982.

Vanhoozer, Kevin J. *Is There a Meaning in This Text? The Bible, the Reader, and the Morality of Literary Knowledge.* Grand Rapids: Zondervan, 1998.

Vartanian, Aram. "Man-Machine from the Greeks to the Computer." *Dictionary of the History of Ideas* 3:131–46.

Veith, Jr., Gene Edward. *Postmodern Times: A Christian Guide to Contemporary Thought and Culture.* Wheaton: Crossway, 1994.

——————. "A Vision, within a Dream, within the Truth: C. S. Lewis as Evangelist to the Postmodernists." In *C. S. Lewis, Lightbearer in the Shadowlands: The Evangelistic Vision of C. S. Lewis,* ed. Angus J. L. Menuge. Wheaton: Crossway, 1997: 367–87.

Walsh, Chad. *C. S. Lewis: Apostle to the Skeptics.* New York: Macmillan, 1949.

—————. *The Literary Legacy of C. S. Lewis.* New York: Harcourt Brace Jovanovich, 1979.

Weaver, Richard. *Ideas Have Consequences.* Chicago: University of Chicago Press, 1948.

White, William Luther. *The Image of Man in C. S. Lewis.* Nashville: Abingdon, 1969.

Wiker, Benjamin. *Moral Darwinism: How We Became Hedonists.* Downers Grove, Ill.: InterVarsity Press, 2002.

Will, George F. "The Nature of Human Nature." *Newsweek* (August 19, 2002): 64.

Williams, Donald T. "A Closer Look at the 'Unorthodox' Lewis." *Christianity Today* (21 December 1979): 24–27.

—————. "A Larger World: C. S. Lewis on Christianity and Literature." *Mythlore* 24:2 (Spring 2004): 45–57.

—————. *Inklings of Reality: Essays toward a Christian Philosophy of Letters.* Toccoa Falls, Ga.: Toccoa Falls College Press, 1996.

—————. "'Is Man a Myth?': Mere Christian Perspectives on the Human." *Mythlore* 23:1 (Summer/Fall 2000): 4–19.

—————. "Lines of Succession: Narnian Hierarchy and Human Relationships." *Touchstone* 18:3 (April 2005): 15–17.

—————. "The Objectivity of Value: Properties, Values, and Moral Reasoning." *The Bulletin of the Evangelical Philosophical Society* 16 (1993): 49–58.

—————. "Reflections from Plato's Cave: Musings on the History of Philosophy" (Evangelical Philosophical Society Presidential Address, 1996). *Philosophia Christi* 20:1 (Spring 1997): 71–82.

—————. "Repairing the Ruins: Thoughts on Christian Higher Education." *Christian Educators Journal* 41:4 (April 2002): 19–21.

—————. Review of *The Pilgrim's Guide: C. S. Lewis and the Art of Witness,* ed. David Mills (Grand Rapids: Eerdmans, 1998) in *The Lamp-Post* 23:2 (Summer 1999): 36–37.

Williams, Donald T., Millard J. Erickson, Kurt Anders, and David C. Clark, "Apologetic Responses to Post-Modernism: A Symposium." *Philosophia Christi* 19:1 (Spring 1996): 1–20; reprint *Evangelical Apologetics: Selected Essays from the 1995 Evangelical Theological Society Convention,* ed. Michael Bauman, David Hall, and Robert Newman. Camp Hill, Penn.: Christian Publications, 1996: 319–41.

Willis, John Randolph. *Pleasure Forevermore: The Theology of C. S. Lewis.* Chicago: Loyola University Press, 1983.

Witherspoon, Alexander M. and Frank J. Warnke. *Seventeenth-Century Prose and Poetry,* 2nd ed. New York: Harcourt Brace Jovanovich, 1982.

Wood, Ralph C. *The Gospel according to Tolkien: Visions of the Kingdom in Middle-Earth.* Louisville: Westminster John Knox Press, 2003.

Wright, Marjorie Evelyn. "The Vision of Cosmic Order in the Oxford Mythmakers." in Charles Huttar, ed., *Imagination and the Spirit: Essays in Literature and the Christian Faith Presented to Clyde S. Kilby.* Grand Rapids: Eerdmans, 1971: 259–76.

Yancey, Philip. "The 'Ample' Man who Saved My Faith: G. K. Chesterton." *Christianity Today,* 3 September 2001: 66–72.

————. "Holy Sex: How It Ravishes Our Souls." *Christianity Today* 47:10 (October 2003): 46–51.

ENDNOTES

Acknowledgments

1. Donald T. Williams, "'Is Man a Myth?' Mere Christian Perspectives on the Human," *Mythlore* 23:1 (Summer/Fall 2000): 4–19.

2. Donald T. Williams, "'Lines of Succession': Narnian Hierarchy and Human Relationships," *Touchstone*, April 2005.

3. Donald T. Williams, "'A Larger World': C. S. Lewis on Christianity and Literature," *Mythlore*, 24:2 (Summer 2004).

4. Donald T. Williams, "The Great Divide: The Church and the Post-Modernist Challenge," *Christian Research Journal* 26:2 (November 2003): 32–41.

Introduction, "Is Man a Myth"

1. Peter Kreeft, *Back to Virtue: Traditional Moral Wisdom for Modern Moral Confusion* (San Francisco: Ignatius, 1992), 31.

2. C. S. Lewis, *A Preface to Paradise Lost* (London: Oxford University Press, 1962), 1. Cf. Colin N. Manlove, *C. S. Lewis: His Literary Achievement* (New York: St. Martin's Press, 1987), 32.

3. For an excellent summary of the arguments pro and con, see Ronald H. Nash, *Life's Ultimate Questions: An Introduction to Philosophy* (Grand Rapids: Zondervan, 1999), 369–84.

4. Marion Montgomery, *The Truth of Things: Liberal Arts and the Recovery of Reality.* (Dallas: Spence Publishing Co., 1999), 177.

5. Francis A. Schaeffer, *Death in the City* (Downers Grove, Ill.: InterVarsity Press, 1969), 98.

6. For further discussion of this argument, see Victor Reppert, *C. S. Lewis's Dangerous Idea: In Defense of the Argument from Reason* (Downers Grove, Ill.: InterVarsity Press, 2003).

7. John Gardner, *On Moral Fiction* (New York: Basic Books, 1978), 8.

8. For some fascinating ruminations on this point, see Karl Heim, *Christian Faith and Natural Science* (San Francisco: Harper & Row, 1953; rpt. Gloucester, Mass.: Peter Smith, 1971), 35ff.

9. George F. Will, "The Nature of Human Nature," *Newsweek,* 19 August 2002, 64.

10. Michel de Montaigne, *Montaigne's Essays and Selected Writings: A Bilingual Edition,* trans. Donald M. Frame (New York: St. Martin's Press, 1963). Cf. the whole argument of Michael Polanyi, *Personal Knowledge: Towards a Post-Critical Philosophy* (New York: Harper & Row, 1964).

11. Quoted in Alexander M. Witherspoon and Frank J. Warnke, *Seventeenth-Century Prose and Poetry,* 2nd ed. (New York: Harcourt Brace Jovanovich, 1982), 339.

12. John Calvin, *Institutes of the Christian Religion,* trans. Henry Beveridge (Grand Rapids: Eerdmans, 1975), 37.

13. Quoted in Colin Brown, *Philosophy and the Christian Faith: An Introduction to the Main Thinkers and Schools of Thought from the Middle Ages to the Present Day* (Downers Grove, Ill.: InterVarsity Press, 1968), 134.

14. Montgomery, *The Truth of Things,* 51.

Chapter 1, "Chesterton and the Everlasting Man"

1. See Mortimer J. Adler, *Ten Philosophical Mistakes* (New York: Macmillan, 1985), 156–66, especially 164.

2. John Gardner, *Grendel* (New York: Vintage Books, 1989), 8.

3. See Francis A. Schaeffer, *Genesis in Space and Time: The Flow of Biblical History* (Downers Grove, Ill.: InterVarsity Press, 1972) for an excellent and balanced treatment of this question.

4. Gardner, *Grendel*, 70–71.

5. G. K. Chesterton, *The Everlasting Man* (New York: Dodd, Mead, and Company, 1925), xxii.

6. For some insightful analysis of the strengths and weaknesses of Chesterton's style, see Maurice Evans, *G. K. Chesterton: The Le Bas Prize Essay* (Cambridge: Cambridge University Press, 1938; rpt. New York: Haskell House, 1972), 134ff.

7. Chesterton, *The Everlasting Man*, xviii.

8. Ibid., 16.

9. Ibid., 15.

10. Clyde S. Kilby, *Christianity and Aesthetics* (Chicago: InterVarsity Press, 1961), 16.

11. Chesterton, *The Everlasting Man*, 21–22.

12. Robert C. Newman, "Scientific Problems for Scientism," *Evangelical Apologetics: Selected Essays from the 1995 Evangelical Theological Society Convention*, ed. Michael Bauman, David Hall, and Robert Newman (Camp Hill, Penn.: Christian Publications, 1996), 245.

13. For an even more comprehensive list of reductionisms, see Peter Kreeft, *C. S. Lewis for the Third Millennium: Six Essays on The Abolition of Man* (San Francisco: Ignatius Press, 1994), 68–69.

14. Richard Weaver, *Ideas Have Consequences* (Chicago: University of Chicago Press, 1948), 6.

15. Ibid., 67.

16. Kreeft, *C. S. Lewis for the Third Millennium;* Owen Barfield, *Owen Barfield on C. S. Lewis,* ed. G. B. Tennyson (Middletown, Conn.: Wesleyan University Press, 1989), 91–92; C. S. Lewis, "The Poison of Subjectivism," *Religion and Life* 12 (1943); rpt. *Christian Reflections,* ed. Walter Hooper (Grand Rapids: Eerdmans, 1967).

17. Barfield, *Owen Barfield on C. S. Lewis,* 82–83.

18. Michael Polyanyi, *The Study of Man* (Chicago: University of Chicago Press, 1959), 47ff; cf. Polanyi, *Personal Knowledge.*

19. Evans, *G. K. Chesterton,* 2ff.

20. Montaigne, *Montaigne's Essays and Selected Writings,* 221.

21. For an interesting argument against our capacity to be reduced to the level of mere animals thus, see Philip Yancey, "Holy Sex: How It Ravishes our Souls," *Christianity Today* 47:10 (October 2003): 46–51.

22. Harry Blamires, *The Christian Mind* (London: S.P.C.K., 1963), 156–57.

23. Chesterton, *The Everlasting Man,* 17.

24. Ibid., 18.

25. Marion Montgomery, *The Truth of Things,* 91.

26. J. P. Moreland, "Philosophical Apologetics, the Church, and Contemporary Culture," *Evangelical Apologetics: Selected Essays from the 1995 Evangelical Theological Society Convention,* ed. Michael Bauman, David Hall, and Robert Newman (Camp Hill, Pa.: Christian Publications, 1996), 11.

27. Chesterton, *The Everlasting Man,* 6.

28. Ibid., 22.

29. For an excellent discussion of the nature of several of these reductionisms, see Michael Bauman, *Pilgrim Theology: Taking the Path of Theological Discovery* (Grand Rapids: Zondervan, 1992), chapters 8–12; on behaviorism, see Francis Schaeffer, *Back to Freedom and Dignity* (Downers Grove, Ill.: InterVarsity Press, 1972); on the postmodern forms, especially as related to literature, good studies include David S. Dockery, ed., *The Challenge of PostModernism: An Evangelical Engagement* (Wheaton: Bridgepoint, 1995); John M. Ellis, *Literature Lost: Social Agendas and the Corruption of the Humanities* (New Haven: Yale University Press, 1997); Gerald Graff, *Literature against Itself: Literary Ideas in Modern Society.* (Chicago: Dee, 1995); Douglas Groothuis, *Truth Decay: Defending Christianity against the Challenges of Postmodernism* (Downers Grove, Ill.: InterVarsity Press,

2000); David Lyle Jeffrey, *People of the Book: Christian Identity and Literary Culture* (Grand Rapids: Eerdmans, 1996); Roger Kimball, *Tenured Radicals: How Politics Has Corrupted Higher Education,* rev. ed. (Chicago: Dee, 1998); Carl Rapp, *Fleeing the Universal: The Critique of Post-Rational Criticism* (Albany: State University of New York Press, 1998); Daniel E. Ritchie, *Reconstructing Literature in an Ideological Age: A Biblical Poetics and Literary Studies from Milton to Burke* (Grand Rapids: Eerdmans, 1996); Kevin J. Vanhoozer, *Is There a Meaning in This Text? The Bible, the Reader, and the Morality of Literary Knowledge* (Grand Rapids: Zondervan, 1998); and Gene Edward Veith Jr., *Postmodern Times: A Christian Guide to Contemporary Thought and Culture* (Wheaton: Crossway, 1994). See also Donald T. Williams, *Inklings of Reality: Essays toward a Christian Philosophy of Letters* (Toccoa Falls, Ga.: Toccoa Falls College Press, 1996), Williams et. al., "Apologetic Responses to Postmodernism: A Symposium." *Philosophia Christi* 19:1 (Spring 1996), 1–20, and this book's Appendix B. Good treatments, particularly of C. S. Lewis in relation to postmodernism, include Gene Edward Veith Jr., "A Vision, within a Dream, within the Truth: C. S. Lewis as Evangelist to the Postmodernists" in Angus J. L. Menuge, ed., *C. S. Lewis, Lightbearer in the Shadowlands: The Evangelistic Vision of C. S. Lewis* (Wheaton: Crossway, 1997), 367–87 and Bruce L. Edwards Jr., *A Rhetoric of Reading: C. S. Lewis's Defense of Western Literacy* (Provo, Utah: Center for the Study of Christian Values in Literature, College of Humanities, Brigham Young University, 1986).

30. Chesterton, *The Everlasting Man*, 158.
31. Ibid., 159.
32. Ibid., xvii.
33. Ibid., 307.
34. Ibid., 20.

Chapter 2, "C. S. Lewis and the Abolition of Man"

1. For a detailed discussion of this point, see Kreeft, *C. S. Lewis for the Third Millennium*, chapter 4.

2. B. F. Skinner, *Beyond Freedom and Dignity* (New York: Bantam, 1971), 191.

3. Joe R. Christopher, *C. S. Lewis,* Twayne's English Authors Series (Boston: G. K. Hall, 1987), 55; cf. Lionel Adey, *C. S. Lewis: Writer, Dreamer, and Mentor* (Grand Rapids: Eerdmans, 1998).

4. Lewis, *The Abolition of Man,* 14.

5. Ibid., 15.

6. J. R. R. Tolkien, *The Two Towers* (New York: Ballantine Books, 1982), 48.

7. Lewis, *The Abolition of Man,* 25.

8. Ibid., 29.

9. C. S. Lewis, *The Four Loves* (New York: Harcourt, Brace & World, 1960), 28.

10. Ibid., 29.

11. Ibid.

12. J. I. Packer, "Living Truth for a Dying World: The Message of C. S. Lewis," *Crux* 34:4 (December 1998): 3–12; reprint *The J. I. Packer Collection,* ed. Alister McGrath (Downers Grove, Ill.: InterVarsity Press, 1999), 277; see also Lewis, "The Poison of Subjectivism," and Donald T. Williams, "The Objectivity of Value: Properties, Values, and Moral Reasoning" in *The Bulletin of the Evangelical Philosophical Society* 16 (1993): 49–58.

13. Lewis, *The Four Loves,* 136–37.

14. Lionel Adey, *C. S. Lewis,* 102–3.

15. For further discussion of this point, see Williams, "The Objectivity of Value."

16. Quoted in Donald X. Burt, *Friendship and Society: An Introduction to Augustine's Practical Philosophy* (Grand Rapids: Eerdmans, 1999), 40.

17. John Milton, *Complete Poems and Major Prose,* ed. Merritt Y. Hughes (Indianapolis: Bobbs-Merrill, 1957), 217.

18. Lewis, *The Abolition of Man,* 29.

19. Cf. Ruby Dunlap, "Common Minds: A Study of Metaphors of Good and Evil across Language Groups," Diss. Tennessee State University, 2002, 93.

20. Lewis, *The Four Loves,* 142.

21. Browne in Witherspoon and Warnke, *Seventeenth-Century Prose and Poetry,* 339.

22. Lewis, *The Abolition of Man,* 34.

23. Ibid., 33–34.

24. Ibid., 35.

25. Ibid., 39; for an enlightening discussion of how similar results ensue when the spirit of the Green Book becomes dominant in literary theory, see Edwards, *A Rhetoric of Reading,* 40–46.

26. Harold O. J. Brown, *The Sensate Culture: Western Civilization Between Chaos and Transformation* (Dallas: Word, 1996), 204.

27. Lewis, *The Abolition of Man,* 77.

28. Ibid., 84–85.

29. Ibid., 54.

30. Ibid., 56.

31. C. S. Lewis, *Out of the Silent Planet* (1938; repr., New York: Simon & Schuster Inc., 1996), 138.

32. *The Abolition of Man,* 56–57.

33. Lewis, Ibid., 86.

34. For a fine discussion of the implications of the Christian worldview for politics, see Gordon H. Clark, *A Christian View of Men and Things* (Grand Rapids: Eerdmans, 1952), 97ff.

35. Brown, *The Sensate Culture,* 84.

36. Lewis, *The Abolition of Man,* 69.

37. Ibid., 72.

38. Ibid., 71.

39. Ibid., 80.

40. Gordon Lewis, "An Integrative Method for Justifying Religious Assertions," in *Evangelical Apologetics: Selected Essays from the 1995 Evangelical Theological Society Convention,* ed. Michael

Bauman, David Hall, and Robert Newman (Camp Hill, Pa.: Christian Publications, 1996), 83.

41. Packer, *Living Truth for a Dying World*, 278.

42. Lewis, *The Abolition of Man*, 83–84.

43. G. K. Chesterton, *Orthodoxy* (Garden City, N.Y.: Doubleday, 1959), 25.

Chapter 3, "J. R. R. Tolkien: Humanity and Faerie"

1. J. R. R. Tolkien, "On Faerie Stories," *The Tolkien Reader* (New York: Ballantine, 1966), 67.

2. Ibid., 54.

3. Williams, *Inklings of Reality*, chapter 1.

4. Cf. Francis A. Schaeffer, *Art and the Bible* (Downers Grove, Ill.: InterVarsity Press, 1973), 34–35.

5. Williams, *Inklings of Reality*, chapter 2.

6. Milton, *Complete Poems and Major Prose*, 720.

7. Weaver, *Ideas Have Consequences*, 150; cf. 158.

8. J. I. Packer, "On from Orr: The Cultural Crisis, Rational Realism, and Incarnational Ontology," *Crux* 32:3 (September 1996): 12–26; reprint *The J. I. Packer Collection*, ed. Alister McGrath (Downers Grove, Ill.: InterVarsity Press, 1999), 251. For an excellent discussion of the nature of several of these reductionisms, see Michael Bauman, *Pilgrim Theology*, chapters 8–12. On behaviorism see Schaeffer, *Back to Freedom and Dignity*. On the postmodern forms, especially as related to literature, good studies include Dockery, *The Challenge of Postmodernism;* Ellis, *Literature Lost;* Graff, *Literature against Itself;* Groothuis, *Truth Decay;* Jeffrey, *People of the Book;* Kimball, *Tenured Radicals;* Rapp, *Fleeing the Universal;* Ritchie, *Reconstructing Literature in an Idealogical Age;* Vanhoozer, *Is There a Meaning in This Text?;* Veith, *Postmodern Times;* see also Williams, "Introduction: Apologetic Responses," *Inklings of Reality,* and Appendix B of this book.

9. Chesterton, *Orthodoxy*, 23.

10. Gardner, *On Moral Fiction*, 174.

11. J. R. R. Tolkien, "Beowulf: The Monsters and the Critics," *Proceedings of the British Academy* 22 (1936); (reprt. *An Anthology of Beowulf Criticism*, ed. Lewis E. Nicholson [Notre Dame, Ind.: Univ. of Notre Dame Press, 1963), 55.

12. Deirdre Greene, "Higher Argument: Tolkien and the Tradition of Vision, Epic, and Prophecy." *Mytholores* 21:2 (Winter 1996): 45.

13. Tolkien, "Faerie Stories," 68.

14. Ibid., 69.

15. J. R. R. Tolkien, *The Letters of J. R. R. Tolkien*, selected and edited by Humphrey Carpenter, with the assistance of Christopher Tolkien (Boston: Houghton Mifflin, 1981), 100.

16. Tolkien, "Faerie Stories," 71.

17. Tolkien, *The Letters of J. R. R. Tolkien*, 101.

18. C. S. Lewis, *Miracles: A Preliminary Study* (New York: Macmillan, 1947), 120.

19. Chesterton, *Orthodoxy*, 49.

20. Tolkien, "Faerie Stories," 4–5.

21. Chesterton, *Orthodoxy*, 78.

Chapter 4, "The Abolition of Hnau"

1. For possible reasons for this other than ignorance or lack of interest, see Christopher, *C. S. Lewis*, 92. Lewis was trying to recapture something of the effect of the medieval worldview described in *The Discarded Image: An Introduction to Medieval and Renaissance Literature,* (Cambridge: Cambridge University Press, 1964).

2. Lewis, *Out of the Silent Planet*, 19.

3. Ibid., 27.

4. Ibid.

5. Ibid., 58.

6. Weaver, *Ideas Have Consequences*, vi.

7. Lewis, *Out of the Silent Planet*, 70.

8. Ibid., 74.

9. Chesterton, *Orthodoxy*, 15.

10. Lewis, *Out of the Silent Planet*, 77.

11. Ibid., 81–82.

12. C. S. Lewis, *The Problem of Pain* (New York: Macmillan, 1967), 54–55.

13. Louis Berkhof, *Systematic Theology*, 4th revised and enlarged ed. (Grand Rapids: Eerdmans, 1939), 246–47.

14. Kenneth Sealer Kantzer, "John Calvin's Theory of the Knowledge of God and the Word of God" (Diss. Harvard, 1950), 313–95; Williams, *Inklings of Reality*, chapter 3.

15. Lewis, *Out of the Silent Planet*, 96.

16. Ibid., 102.

17. Lewis, *The Problem of Pain*, 68.

18. Lewis, *Out of the Silent Planet*, 102–3.

19. To see what a sophisticated view of the epistemological importance of metaphor that avoids falling into this dilemma might look like, see C. S. Lewis, "Bluspels and Flalansferes: A Semantic Nightmare" *Selected Literary Essays*, ed. Walter Hooper (Cambridge: Cambridge University Press, 1969), 251–65; cf. Dunlap, "Common Minds."

20. Lewis, *Out of the Silent Planet*, 120.

21. Ibid., 138.

22. Lewis, *Perelandra*, 56.

23. Ibid., 56.

24. Quoted in Witherspoon and Warnke, *Seventeenth Century Prose and Poetry*, 69.

25. Lewis, *Perelandra*, 65.

26. Lewis, *The Four Loves*, 79.

27. Marjorie Evelyn Wright, "The Vision of Cosmic Order in the Oxford Mythmakers," in Charles Huttar, ed., *Imagination and*

the Spirit: Essays in Literature and the Christian Faith Presented to Clyde S. Kilby (Grand Rapids: Eerdmans, 1971), 259ff.

28. Lewis, *Perelandra*, 68.

29. John Milton, *Paradise Lost*, III.99.

30. C. S. Lewis, "De Descriptione Temporum," *Selected Literary Essays*, ed. Walter Hooper (Cambridge: Cambridge University Press, 1969), 12–14.

31. Burt, *Friendship and Society*, 3.

32. Lewis, *Perelandra*, 69–70.

33. Ibid., 130.

34. C. S. Lewis, *The Weight of Glory* (pub. in England under the title *Transposition and Other Addresses*) (New York: Macmillan, 1949), 15.

35. Lewis, *Perelandra*, 205–6.

36. Tolkien, *The Letters of J. R. R. Tolkien*, 342.

37. Schaeffer, *Back to Freedom and Dignity*, 29.

38. C. S. Lewis, *The Screwtape Letters and Screwtape Proposes a Toast* (New York: Macmillan, 1961), 33.

39. Lewis, *That Hideous Strength*, 71.

40. Ibid., 87.

41. Ibid., 178.

42. Ibid., 203.

43. Packer, "On from Orr," 251.

44. Lewis, *That Hideous Strength*, 255.

45. Ibid., 256.

46. Compare Weaver's discussion of the role of "sentiment" in *Ideas Have Consequences*.

47. Lewis, *That Hideous Strength*, 296.

48. Ibid., 295.

49. Ibid.

50. Ibid.

51. Ibid., 310.

52. Ibid., 337.

53. Ibid., 371.

54. See Thomas C. Oden, "Christian Apologetics in a non-Christian World," *Evangelical Apologetics: Selected Essays from the 1995 Evangelical Theological Society Convention,* ed. Michael Bauman, David Hall, and Robert Newman (Camp Hill, Penn.: Christian Publications, 1996), 280–83.

55. Lewis, *That Hideous Strength,* 378.

Chapter 5, "The Abolition of Talking Beasts"

1. Colin N. Manlove, *The Chronicles of Narnia: The Patterning of a Fantastic World* (New York: Twayne Publishers, 1993).

2. For a masterful treatment of this issue, see Peter J. Schakel, "The 'Correct' Order for Reading the Chronicles of Narnia," *Mythlore* 23:2 (Spring 2001): 4–14.

3. C. S. Lewis, *Surprised by Joy: The Shape of My Early Life* (New York: Harcourt, Brace, and World, 1955), 7, 16–18, 72–73, etc.

4. C. S. Lewis, *The Voyage of the Dawn Treader* (New York: HarperCollins, 1978), 226.

5. Ibid., 168.

6. Manlove, *The Chronicles of Narnia,* 113.

7. C. S. Lewis, *The Lion, the Witch, and the Wardrobe* (New York: HarperCollins, 1978), 87.

8. Ibid., 87–88.

9. C. S. Lewis, *The Silver Chair* (New York: HarperCollins, 1978), 238.

10. C. S. Lewis, *Prince Caspian* (New York: HarperCollins, 1978), 71.

11. C. S. Lewis, *The Horse and His Boy* (New York: HarperCollins, 1978), 33.

12. C. S. Lewis, *Mere Christianity* (New York: Macmillan, 1943); For a refreshing exception to the pattern see John Piper and Wayne Grudem, eds., *Recovering Biblical Manhood and Womanhood: A Response to Evangelical Feminism* (Wheaton: Crossway, 1991), which

often combines strong biblical exegesis with a good understanding of these issues.

13. Lewis, *The Horse and His Boy,* 240.

14. C. S. Lewis, *The Magician's Nephew* (New York: HarperCollins, 1978), 165.

15. Ibid.

16. Lewis, *The Horse and His Boy,* 146.

17. Lewis, *Prince Caspian,* 73.

18. Lewis, *The Magician's Nephew,* 140.

19. Ibid., 136–38.

20. Lewis, Ibid., 139.

21. Lewis, *Prince Caspian,* 128.

22. Lewis, *The Lion, the Witch, and the Wardrobe,* 88.

23. Lewis, *The Voyage of the Dawn Treader,* 97.

24. Lewis, "Eden's Courtesy." *Poems,* ed. Walter Hooper (New York: Harcourt Brace Jovanovich, 1964): 98.

25. Quoted in Nash, *Life's Ultimate Questions,* 351.

26. Edmund Spenser, *The Faerie Queene,* 2 vols., ed. J. C. Smith (Oxford: Oxford University Press, 1909), II.xii.87.

27. Lewis, *The Magician's Nephew,* 203.

28. Lewis, *The Horse and His Boy,* 230.

29. Ibid., 8.

30. Lewis, *The Voyage of the Dawn Treader,* 231.

31. Lewis, *The Silver Chair,* 190–91.

32. Lewis, *Surprised by Joy;* cf. Barfield, *Owen Barfield on C. S. Lewis,* 56.

33. C. S. Lewis, *The Last Battle* (New York: HarperCollins, 1978), 213.

34. Ibid., 228.

35. Ibid., 87.

36. Lewis, *The Voyage of the Dawn Treader,* 270.

37. Lewis, *Prince Caspian,* 232–33.

Chapter 6, "The Everlasting Hobbit"

1. See G. C. Berkouwer, *Man: The Image of God,* Studies in Dogmatics, vol. 8 (Grand Rapids: Eerdmans, 1962) for example; contrast Philip Edgcumbe Hughes, *The True Image: The Origin and Destiny of Man in Christ* (Grand Rapids: Eerdmans, 1989; reprint, Eugene, Ore.: Wipf & Stock, 2001), who does a better job of sticking with the text.

2. Williams, *Inklings of Reality,* chapter 1.

3. For analysis of some of the details of that process, see T. A. Shippey, "Creation from Philology in The Lord of the Rings," in Mary Salu and Robert T. Farrell, eds., *J. R. R. Tolkien, Scholar and Storyteller: Essays in Memoriam* (Ithaca: Cornell University Press, 1979), 286–316.

4. Warren H. Lewis, *Brothers and Friends: The Diaries of Major Warren Hamilton Lewis,* ed. Clyde S. Kilby and Marjorie Lamp Mead (New York: Ballantine, 1982), 259.

5. Gardner, *On Moral Fiction,* 194.

6. Lewis, *The Voyage of the Dawn Treader,* 270.

7. Derek S. Brewer, "The Lord of the Rings as Romance," in Salu and Farrell, eds. *J. R. R. Tolkien, Scholar and Storyteller,* 249–64; William Dowie, "The Gospel of Middle Earth according to J. R. R. Tolkien," in Salu and Farrell, eds., *J. R. R. Tolkien, Scholar and Storyteller,* 265–85.

8. Shippey, "Creation from Philology in The Lord of the Rings," 315.

9. Tom Shippey, "Tolkien and the Gawain Poet," *Mythlore* 21:2 (Winter 1996): 213–19.

10. J. R. R. Tolkien, *The Fellowship of the Ring* (New York: Ballantine Books, 1982), 20.

11. Verlyn Flieger, "Fantasy and Reality: J. R. R. Tolkien's World and the Fairy Story Essay," *Mythlore* 22:3 (Winter 1999): 9.

12. J. R. R. Tolkien, *The Silmarillion* (Boston: Houghton Mifflin Co., 1977), 17.

13. Ibid., 18.

14. Tolkien, *The Fellowship of the Ring*, 102.

15. Tolkien, *The Silmarillion*, 19.

16. Ibid., 41.

17. Ibid.

18. Tolkien, *The Fellowship of the Ring*, 7.

19. Tolkien, *The Two Towers*, 77.

20. Tolkien, *The Silmarillion*, 42.

21. For a discussion of a similar idea in Chesterton, see Evans, *G. K. Chesterton*, 42.

22. J. R. R. Tolkien, *The Return of the King* (New York: Ballantine Books, 1982), 352.

23. Tolkien, *The Two Towers*, 199.

24. J. R. R. Tolkien, *The Hobbit* (New York: Ballantine Books, 1982), 303.

25. Tolkien, *The Fellowship of the Ring*, 81.

26. Ibid., 472.

27. Tolkien, *The Two Towers*, 48.

28. Ibid., 43–44.

29. Ibid., 336.

30. Tolkien, *The Return of the King*, 284.

31. Ibid., 204–5.

32. Brewer, "The Lord of the Rings as Romance," 258.

33. Quoted in Russell Noyes, ed., *English Romantic Poetry and Prose* (New York: Oxford University Press, 1956), 981.

34. Tolkien, *The Return of the King*, 164.

35. Ibid., 261.

36. Cf. Verlyn Flieger, "A Question of Time," *Mythlore* 16:3 (Spring 1990): 5–8.

37. Brewer, "The Lord of the Rings as Romance," 261.

38. Tolkien, *The Return of the King*, 282.

39. Ibid., 389.

40. Dowie, "The Gospel of Middle Earth according to J. R. R. Tolkien," 282–83.

41. Dwayne Thorpe, "Tolkien's Elvish Craft," *Mythlore* 21:2 (Winter 1996): 316.

42. Tolkien, *The Return of the King*, 346–53.

Conclusion

1. Williams, "Conclusion," chapter 1, *Inklings of Reality*.

2. James Patrick, *The Magdalen Metaphysicals: Idealism and Orthodoxy at Oxford, 1901–1945* (Macon, Ga.: Mercer University Press, 1985), 131.

3. Brown, *The Sensate Culture*, 237.

Appendix A, "Stories and Stock Responses"

1. Roger Houston Smith, Patches of Godlight: The Pattern of Thought of C. S. Lewis (Athens: University of Ga. Press, 1981), x.

2. Peter Schakel, *Reason and Imagination in C. S. Lewis: A Study of 'Till We Have Faces* (Grand Rapids: Eerdmans, 1984), xi.

3. Norman Reed Cary, *Christian Criticism in the Twentieth Century* (Port Washington, N.Y.: Kennicat Press, 1975), 16.

4. C. S. Lewis, "Christianity and Culture," *Theology* 40 (March 1940); reprinted in *Christian Reflections,* ed. Walter Hooper (Grand Rapids: Eerdmans, 1967): 15.

5. Ibid., 14.

6. C. S. Lewis, "Christianity and Literature," *Rehabilitations and Other Essays* (Oxford, Oxford University Press, 1939); reprint *Christian Reflections,* ed. Walter Hooper (Grand Rapids: Eerdmans, 1967), 10.

7. For an excellent treatment of the importance of this theme in Lewis's life, see David Mills, ed., *The Pilgrim's Guide: C. S. Lewis and the Art of Witness* (Grand Rapids: Eerdmans, 1998), especially Christopher Mitchell, "Bearing the Weight of Glory: The Cost of C. S. Lewis's Witness," 3–14; Harry Blamires, "Teaching the

Universal Truth: C. S. Lewis among the Intellectuals," 15–26; and Bruce Edwards, "A Thoroughly Converted Man: C. S. Lewis in the Public Square," 27–39.

8. Lewis, "Christianity and Culture," 12.

9. Thomas Erskine of Linlathen, quoted in Lewis, *Miracles*, 10.

10. Lewis, "Christianity and Culture," 20.

11. Ibid., 20–21.

12. Ibid., 21.

13. Ibid.

14. Ibid., 22.

15. Stephen Thorson, "'Knowledge' in C. S. Lewis's Post-Conversion Thought: His Epistemological Method," *SEVEN: An Anglo-American Literary Review*, 9 (1988): 111.

16. C. S. Lewis, "On Three Ways of Writing for Children," The Library Association, *Proceedings, Papers, and Summaries of Discussions at the Bournemouth Conference, 29 April to 2 May 1952*; reprint, *Of Other Worlds*, ed. Walter Hooper (New York: Harcourt, Brace, Jovanovich, 1964), 29.

17. C. S. Lewis, "The Language of Religion," Address from ca. 1953, first published in *Christian Reflections*, 133.

18. Ibid.

19. C. S. Lewis, *An Experiment in Criticism* (Cambridge: Cambridge University Press, 1961), 140.

20. C. S. Lewis, "An Expostulation against Too Many Writers of Science Fiction," *Magazine of Fantasy and Science Fiction*, 16 (June 1959): 47; reprint, *Poems*, ed. Walter Hooper (New York: Harcourt Brace Jovanovich, 1964), 58.

21. C. S. Lewis, "Sometimes Fairy Stories May Say Best What's to be Said," *New York Times Book Review*, Children's Book Section, November 1956; reprint, *Of Other Worlds*, 37.

22. Lewis, *Surprised by Joy*, 181; for a fuller discussion of Lewis's views on imagination, see Peter J. Schakel, *Imagination and the Arts*

in C. S. Lewis: Journeying to Narnia and Other Worlds (Columbia: University of Missouri Press, 2002), especially chapters 1 and 9.

23. C. S. Lewis, *Pilgrim's Regress,* 11; cf. Thorson, "Knowledge," 111.

24. For some interesting development of this fact, see R. D. Stock, "The Tao and the Objective Room: A Pattern in C. S. Lewis's Novels," *Christian Scholar's Review* 9:3 (1980): 256–66.

25. Schakel, *Imagination and the Arts in C. S. Lewis,* 18.

26. Lewis, *The Voyage of the Dawn Treader,* 270.

27. Luci Shaw, "C. S. Lewis: The Light in the Kilns," *Christianity and Literature* 52:1 (Autumn 2002): 34.

28. Lewis, *Preface to Paradise Lost,* 55.

29. T. S. Eliot, "Tradition and the Individual Talent," *Selected Essays* (New York: Harcourt, Brace, & Co., 1950), 7.

30. T. S. Eliot, "The Social Function of Poetry," 1943; reprint, *On Poetry and Poets* (New York: Noonday Press, 1961), 9.

31. C. S. Lewis, "A Confession," originally published as "Spartan Nactus," *Punch* 227 (1 December 1954): 685; reprint, *Poems,* ed. Walter Hooper (New York: Harcourt Brace Jovanovich, 1964), 1.

32. Charles Huttar, "A Lifelong Love Affair with Language: C. S. Lewis's Poetry," *Word and Story in C. S. Lewis,* ed. Peter J. Schakel and Charles A. Huttar (Columbia: University of Missouri Press, 1991), 96.

33. Ibid., 97.

34. Lewis, "A Confession," 1.

35. Lewis, *A Preface to Paradise Lost,* 54.

36. Huttar, "A Lifelong Love Affair with Language," 99.

37. Ibid., 97.

38. Lewis, *The Abolition of Man,* 14.

39. For useful further discussion of how "stock responses" relate to the natural law of *Mere Christianity* and the *Tao* of *The Abolition of Man,* see Stock, "The Tao and the Objective Room."

40. Lewis, *A Preface to Paradise Lost,* 57.

41. Lewis, "On Three Ways of Writing for Children," 31.

42. Eliot, "Tradition and the Individual Talent," 6.

43. Lewis, *Surprised by Joy,* 207; for the history of Barfield's influence on Lewis, see Stephen Thorson, "Lewis and Barfield on Imagination," *Mythlore,* 17:2 (Winter 1990): 12–18; "Lewis and Barfield on Imagination, Part II," *Mythlore,* 17:3 (Spring 1991): 16–21.

44. Lewis, *Surprised by Joy,* 208.

45. C. S. Lewis, "On the Reading of Old Books," Preface to St. Athanasius, *The Incarnation of the Word of God,* trans. A Religious of C.S.M.V. Bles, 1944; reprint, *God in the Dock,* ed. Walter Hooper (Grand Rapids: Eerdmans, 1970), 201.

46. Ibid., 202.

47. Thorson, "'Knowledge' in C. S. Lewis's Post-Conversion Thought," 111.

48. C. S. Lewis, "Lilies That Fester," in *The World's Last Night and Other Essays* (New York: Harcourt, Brace & World, 1952): 31–49; cf. *An Experiment in Criticism* (Cambridge: Cambridge University Press, 1961).

49. See Williams, especially *Inklings of Reality,* introduction and chapters 1, 2, 7; and Edwards *in toto* for extended treatment of this theme.

INDEX OF NAMES

INDEX OF CHARACTERS

INDEX OF SUBJECTS

211